CHANGING TIMES

S. D. Jones
Lucy Jane Bledsoe

FEARON EDUCATION
500 Harbor Boulevard
Belmont, California

Simon & Schuster Supplementary Education Group

SPELLBINDERS™
FEARON'S FINEST FICTION

Cover Illustrator: Terry Hoff

ISBN 0-8224-2808-3
Library of Congress Catalog Card Number: 90-82220
Printed in the United States of America
1. 9 8 7 6 5 4 3 2 1

Contents

Fortune in Men's Eyes

S. D. Jones

CHAPTER

1

On the night of August 21, 1853, Matthew Wilder threw a little party for himself—out on the trail. He lit a cheerful campfire, ate a meal of beans and corn, and sang a song to his horse.

It was a night he didn't want to forget. Not because any great event of man or nature had taken place. No, this was much more personal. He felt good about surviving three whole weeks away from his parents. And he wasn't even homesick.

It was a cause for celebration. A landmark of his own independence. The fire seemed brighter and warmer than any he had ever lit. The meal seemed tastier than any he had prepared before it. And the song ... . well, his horse didn't seem to mind it any.

The stars he could see in the Western sky that night numbered in the millions. Matthew lay awake for an hour, counting nearly 80 shooting stars. He figured he was a very lucky young man.

Matthew thought back to all the people he had come across in the past three weeks. His father told him he would not meet a soul. He'd said that if the wolves didn't get him the loneliness and boredom would. But it was not like that—not like that at all. The borderless highways of the plains that would one day be Colorado and Wyoming were alive with travelers. Many of them were just like himself. But there were also fortune hunters, runaways, prospectors, trappers, and Indian scouts.

The travelers told of fortunes won and lost. Of gold and silver running like rivers that are just out of reach. But all the woe, misery and failure in their adventures did not worry Matthew Wilder.

Most of the storytellers showed signs of being drunkards, or weak fools wanting only a good time. He was different.

If there was any gold to find, he knew he would find it. He'd stake his claim and reap the rewards. He would ride back into town a hero, a rich hero at that. And his father, mother, and all his friends would take notice. No, he was not worried about defeat. If anything, the prospectors' mistakes served as lessons.

All together it had been a grand three weeks. The days may have been hot and long. And at times the ride was tiring and the trail rough. But he was on his own. And the world was opening up before him. The west itself seemed to be welcoming him. The voices in the wind seemed to sing, "Take my hills and valleys, my rivers and my gold. They have been waiting since the dawn of time . . . just for you." And on this night, the world *was* Matthew Wilder's, and he cherished it.

Matthew thought back to the days just before he had left home. Compared to the way he felt now, those days seemed like a bad dream. They were filled with pain and sorrow, goodbyes and heartaches.

He remembered that it had been a warm summer day when he and his sister Hattie had said goodbye. But it was Hattie who was leaving that day—not Matthew.

They had set out on a picnic, under the oak tree down by the stream. Just Hattie and Matthew and their dog, Wigwam. Hattie had made a plateful of fried chicken and they'd brought along some lemonade. Hattie had to keep Wigwam from making grabs at the chicken. Matthew could still hear her voice:

"No, Wigwam. Git," she snapped at the naughty mutt. "That dog! It was you who taught him to beg and steal from the table, Matthew," Hattie said. But Matthew wasn't listening to his sister. He was staring back toward their house. Hattie took note of his daydream.

"Matthew? Are you okay?" she asked him.

"I don't want you leaving," Matthew said. "I don't know why you have to do this."

"Because I'm getting married, silly," she said.

"You have lots of men who want to marry you right here in town," Matthew said. "Why do you have to go marry some man from South Carolina?"

"You know I have to get away from here, Matthew," she said.

"You don't love us. Me, Mamma, or Pa."

"That's not true and you know it," Hattie answered. She shook him and made him look her in the eye. "I'm not trying to run away from you. I *love* my family. I'll miss you more than a coyote misses a full moon. But Thomas is a wealthy man. He owns a business back east. He's well respected. Everyone knows him. This is my chance to have all the things I've ever read or heard about."

"Do you love him?" Matthew asked.

"Oh, it's not all that simple," she told her brother. "You'll understand when you're a little older. There's more to marrying than just love. You have to respect the person. You should admire what he does and what he stands for, too."

"Well . . ." Matthew said. "It wouldn't hurt to like him a little, too. You've done a lot of talking about Mr. Thomas Pryce of South Carolina. But with all your talk, you haven't ever once mentioned liking him. I may only be 20 years old, but I know that much. I surely do."

"Oh that's enough, Matthew," Hattie said and turned away. "Let's just eat and stop all this talking. I worked like a mule making this picnic for us. Let's just have a good time."

So they decided not to talk anymore about Thomas Pryce or South Carolina.

Matthew crunched down hard on the chicken, as though he were gobbling up all his fears and anger.

After a few minutes he almost forgot that in two hours Hattie would be gone— maybe forever. When would he ever get to travel back East to see his sister? The East held no charm or mystery for Matthew. Hattie had always dreamed of the fine life in a big city. Matthew dreamed of mountains, wide open spaces, and gold. This was why he decided to head west as soon as he could. He'd leave Hatfield's Bluff soon after Hattie did.

Their time at the picnic flew by. Soon the sun began to sink lower in the western sky.

"Lordy!" Hattie suddenly yelled, scaring the dog. "Look at the sun. Why it must be close to four."

Sure enough, almost as soon as Hattie said those words, the church bells struck four o'clock. The bells only rang twice a week: on Sundays for worship, and later at four, when the weekly stage heading east was set to leave town.

"Hurry, Matthew. Grab what you can. Just scoop everything up. Hurry. I'll be late. I'll miss the stage," she cried.

"Wouldn't that be too bad."

"Matthew Wilder, don't sass me. If I miss that stage, I'll . . ."

Before Matthew could gather up the chicken, his sister was running down the road toward town. Wigwam followed quickly on her trail.

"Hattie, wait!" Matthew cried.

"Hurry!" she cried as she and the dog disappeared around the bend.

Matthew left the rest of the chicken for the birds. He just tucked the basket under his arm and hustled toward town as best he could.

When he arrived, his mother and father were already there. They were standing by the stage, hugging and fussing over Hattie. Matthew could not help but notice that Thomas Pryce stood by, tall and erect. He seemed almost proud that he was taking Hattie away.

"We gotta move out," the stage driver yelled. The man scrambled to his place and took the reins of the six-horse team.

"Hattie!" Matthew cried out and waved. He dropped the basket and raced as fast as he could to her side. He gave her one last hug.

"Take care of yourself," Matthew said.

Then with a little more command in his voice he addressed Mr. Thomas Pryce. "You take care of her, too."

"That I will, son," came the gentleman's reply.

"Oh, Matthew," Hattie said, hugging her brother again, long and hard. "I'll be fine. You know I'll be fine. I'll be with family. Well, almost family," she added.

Thomas Pryce was a business partner of the Dunfords, Matthew and Hattie's cousins. But that was of little comfort to Matthew. He knew little about these cousins. He had never met the Dunfords and didn't care to.

Finally Hattie let go of Matthew and stood tall. But there were tears in her eyes. "My. I don't know when I've had so much fussing done over me," she said. "I'll try to make it last." And in what seemed like a second, Hattie Wilder was gone.

Matthew could still hear her words floating along the night wind. It hurt him to think about Hattie. The passing weeks had not lessened his sadness. How could his sister have gone off with that businessman from South Carolina? He wondered where she was tonight. He wondered how her journey was coming. Was she home yet? Was she happy? He might never know.

Finally the deep sorrow of his thoughts gave way to the more powerful urge for sleep. He drifted off looking forward to another adventuresome day on the trail. But when he woke at dawn, it was not the bright morning sun that first greeted him. Nor was it the crystal blue sky. Matthew awoke to a shotgun aimed right between his eyes.

2

At the other end of the gun stood a tall, muscular black man. Matthew could not clearly make out his face. The sun was behind the man, casting a dark shadow over his brow. He wore a wide brimmed hat set low on his forehead. The man said nothing, but waited for Matthew to get up.

This is not how Matthew wanted to begin his day. And certainly not how he wanted to end it. "Morning," he finally said meekly.

The black man said nothing.

Matthew cautiously rose to his elbows. "Coffee?" he asked.

The black man nodded. But he kept the gun right between Matthew's eyes.

"I'll need to get up in order to make it, you know?" Matthew said.

The black man took a cautious step back as Matthew stood and stretched. Since the beginning of his journey, Matthew had met lots of men with guns. He felt it didn't pay to be scared of them. The men could read your fears and take advantage of them. "Help me get this fire going," Matthew said. But the black man hesitated. "Look. I don't mind sharing what I have with you," Matthew said firmly. "But you're going to have to help, or you can just git."

The black man, surprised at the show of courage, let the gun drop to his side.

"That's better," said Matthew. And for the first time, he got a good look at the man. He seemed to be about ten years older than Matthew. He was dirty and tired, and his clothes didn't fit well. There were holes in his buckskin shirt and his boots were shoddy and worn.

Matthew began to wonder if the man was an outlaw. He had the same wild look in his eyes that Matthew had seen in so many other travelers. But in the others he also saw fear. In this man he saw no fear. The black man's eyes were calm. Or maybe they were just empty—lacking any feeling or emotion.

"What's your name, friend?" Matthew asked. When he didn't get an answer, he went on. "Mine's Wilder. Matthew Wilder. People call me Matt."

The black man finally set his gun beside a stone and threw some wood into a pile. "The name's Zeke," the man said in a grave whisper.

"Zeke what?"

"Just Zeke."

All right, Matthew thought. If he wants to be that way, let him. I don't need company.

After a few moments, Matthew got the fire going and brewed up some coffee. The two men sat in silence for about a half an hour, slowly drinking their coffee.

Finally Matthew gathered up his few possessions and started to saddle up. Zeke looked up at him. But he didn't move an inch from his spot by the fire.

"I'm heading for the trail," Matthew said in a stiff voice. "You're welcome to ride along. Or you can stay here. It's all the same to me."

Zeke slowly got up. He threw the rest of his coffee away, and put out the fire. Then he saddled up, too, and turned his horse around.

"Guess I'll ride along for a spell," he finally said. "You seem harmless—and you ain't so curious as to be annoying."

In anger Matthew started to say something, but then changed his mind. Instead he spurred his horse forward, and mumbled, "Suit yourself."

The two men rode side by side without a word for several miles. Finally Matthew decided to make one more effort to get Zeke to open up. Then he'd quit trying— and ride off on his own at the first opportunity.

"Where you headed?" Matthew asked. "California's my spot. That's where I'm going. Near as I figure, another day's ride and I should join up with a wagon train at Miller's Ridge. That suits me fine. Past Miller's Ridge it's Indian territory. You don't want to ride alone through there."

Matthew was hoping his own enthusiasm might loosen Zeke's tongue. "Plan to find gold in California. People have been getting rich for years there. Now it's my turn."

But the more Matthew talked, the more he realized what he had suspected for some time. It wasn't common to see a black man riding by himself in the

Colorado Territory. And one that looked like Zeke was probably running from something.

"You been riding by yourself for a long time?" Matthew asked.

"A ways."

"You must have passed through Indian country."

"Yeah. Some. They don't seem to mind seeing a black man. Not as afraid of a black man as they are of white men."

"You're right there," Matthew replied. "My pa was a trapper. Used to trade with Indians. But they liked him. My mamma was half Indian, too. That makes me part Indian, you know."

Matthew continued to talk, trying to make conversation with the man riding beside him. But the more Matthew looked into Zeke's eyes, the more he realized the truth.

"You're a runaway, aren't you?" Matthew said at last. Zeke said nothing. But for the first time since he'd met him, Matthew saw fear in Zeke's eyes. What was strangely missing before now seemed to be written all over his face.

"You're a slave," Matthew said. He even surprised himself as he heard the words escape his lips. "A runaway."

Zeke suddenly stopped his horse in its tracks. He looked at Matthew with a fierce gaze. "I am," he said simply.

Matthew knew about runaway slaves, though he had never seen one before. He couldn't remember hearing of anyone making it out this far. Of course he had seen plenty of other black men before. Old Jake Granger had some Negro help ranching his lands. Matthew had never thought of them as slaves though. And it didn't cross his mind now to take advantage of Zeke's situation.

"I don't aim to make trouble for you, friend," said Matthew.

"I got a price on my head," Zeke replied. It was almost as if he were taunting him to try something. "Five hundred dollars."

"Ha," said Matthew. "I'll make that much in my first month prospecting." But as he thought about it, the price seemed quite high for an ordinary slave.

"That's a lot of money for a slave," said Matthew.

"Yep," said Zeke. Then he tugged on the reins and clicked his horse forward. "But the price is just about right to put on the head of a *murderer*."

Matthew was truly frightened for the first time since he'd left home. Here he was, in the middle of nowhere, riding with a murderer. After Zeke had made that statement, he had said nothing. He simply rode on, as though the matter was closed. Matthew thought it best not to bring it up again. But he watched Zeke with a new found suspicion. He also unlatched the strap that held his six-shooter in place.

It was not until supper time that the two men spoke about it again.

"I'm hungry," Zeke finally said.

"Well," Matthew began, "I got enough food to last one person till Miller's Ridge. I don't know how much farther you plan on riding along. But if it's all the way there, you best figure out some way to help feed us. I'm not your mess tent, you know."

Zeke stopped his horse and stared at Matthew. Immediately, Matthew's blood ran cold. Who had Matthew thought he was talking to—an old friend? This was a man who said he was a murderer! Matthew thought of several ways of apologizing. But before he could voice a single one, Zeke took off like a bolt of lightning.

"Hey!" Matthew cried. "Wait." But Zeke could not hear past the thundering of his horse's hooves. He was heading for a grove of trees about a mile away.

Matthew did not know what to do. Would Zeke be back? Had he really run off, angered or somehow hurt by what Matthew had said? Matthew couldn't make up his mind whether to ride off or follow Zeke. So he chose the middle ground. He found a cluster of rocks and decided to wait in what little shade they cast.

"I'll give him half an hour to get himself back here," he announced. "Then he can ride the wind for all I care."

A few moments later, Matthew heard a gunshot. He stood to see if he could make out the direction of the sound. As he did, he saw Zeke racing back toward him. When Zeke's horse got closer, Matthew saw there was an animal strapped to its back. He shielded his eyes against the light of the bright sun. As he did, he saw a huge jack rabbit drop. It landed at his feet.

"That do it?" asked Zeke. He dismounted and started to gather firewood. "You ever skin a rabbit?"

"Sure."

"Well, you'd better get to it. I'll be done with the fire in no time." Without another word, Zeke began building their fire for the night.

"I'm sorry Zeke," Matthew said. "I just meant that you needed to help—"

"That's what I've done, haven't I? You told me to jump, and I jumped."

Matthew thought it best to leave well enough alone. The two men worked at their chores for a while. Finally Zeke looked up at Matthew. "Why did your family let you go off into country like this?" he asked.

"Oh, well, my mamma and pa didn't have much say in this. Sometimes a man has to set off to see things for himself.

And it's no one else's business, is it?"

Zeke laughed. "You ran away, too, didn't you?"

Matthew looked truly hurt. "What?"

"No father or mother lets a son just up and drift away when he feels it's time. Especially the kind of folks the son still calls mamma and pa."

"I told them of my plans," Matthew said.

"I reckon that's true," Zeke said. "You told them you had some big ideas to go off and conquer the world. But I vow you didn't tell them *when* you were doing all this. Nope. One night you were there, and the next you were gone. And half the kitchen stock with you."

Matthew hated to have the truth held up to him so boldly. He had just spent three weeks telling himself that his folks must have known it was coming. Now suddenly it all seemed like a big lie. He *had* run away from home. He had left without a single goodbye. And just as quickly as the truth fell on him, Matthew felt homesick.

Zeke asked, "Why'd you do it?"

"I don't know."

"Don't you?"

"My sister left home. She got married, moved back east. After that, I guess I just felt like there was nothing left for me. Me and Hattie used to be real close. As long as she was around, I didn't have to think about my life. With her gone, everything just seemed like chores. My pa's a tracker, a trader. He deals in furs, pelts, things like that. I helped him out."

"Won't he miss you?" asked Zeke.

"Nah. My pa always said that Hattie had a better head for business. That's the truth. She's smart as a whip. Me . . . I just always abided it. I put in my time helping my pa, but I didn't have much heart for it. He'll get along fine without me.

"Anyway," Matthew continued, "there wasn't much reason to hang around anymore. But I'll be back someday. Then I'll buy the town I grew up in and everything in it. And then I can give my mamma a rest. She's lived a dozen lives all rolled into one. I swear I'll go back, Zeke, you'll see."

Zeke just said, "I believe you boy. I do believe you."

"How about you?" Matthew asked.

"Me?"

"Yeah. I mean, why did *you* run? Did they beat you? I'll bet I know. I bet somebody whipped you. And you hit him back and accidentally killed him, right?"

Zeke watched the fire catch and the flames leap through the dead wood. He thought about telling Matthew a lie. Just to keep the young man from asking any more questions. But the truth of it was, Zeke wanted to get it off his chest. Lord knows he had no one else to tell. No one else had even bothered to ask.

"It ain't the beating. You can take that," he said. "You hurt, you bleed. But the bleeding stops. The hurt goes away. God built men to take it. And it's not the food— the stuff you wouldn't feed your pigs— you get used to it. You even thank the Lord for it. It keeps you going. And it's not being cussed out or laughed at either. All that you can take. It's none of that. But it's something else just as real, but harder to say.

"At first you're fine. There's this little voice inside you that tells you how good you are. Even when everyone else cusses you. When life seems bad today, the little voice says things will be better tomorrow.

It tells you to sing when you feel like crying. It tells you to turn away when you feel like fighting back.

"But then something happens. You wake up one morning and you notice the little voice isn't there anymore. And you get real quiet. You listen for it, but it's gone. You work and you can't sing. You hurt, and you don't feel better. You get hit, and you want to hit back. Because the voice inside you is missing. And when that happens, you start to disappear.

"So I ran away all right. I ran away to try to find myself and that little voice inside me. It's out there somewhere. It just got lost, buried like your gold. But I aim to dig it up. And then maybe I can ride back into *my* town someday. If I can, I'll be richer than any man alive."

Matthew could not look at Zeke. He just stared into the fire. He wondered what it was like to be a slave. He tried to imagine it. But he couldn't do it.

Matthew had never had a savage beating. He'd never lost that little voice inside. Matthew knew what Zeke meant about that. He had a little voice inside him, too. But his voice was different from the one Zeke had, he was sure. For

Matthew, the little voice was what was pushing him to California to find gold. For Zeke, the little voice was what had kept him alive. It was a space between them that could never be bridged by any talk. And yet, somehow, Matthew felt a closeness to this stranger.

They cooked the rabbit and ate it heartily. It was tough, but it tasted good. Later, Matthew and Zeke sat before the fire and listened to some poor coyote crying to the rising moon.

Matthew felt at ease once more, as though things would be all right. He hoped Zeke would ride on with him toward Miller's Ridge. But there was still a matter that kept eating away at Matthew. And it kept him from truly trusting the man who sat across from the leaping flames.

"Zeke?"

"Yeah."

"Who did you kill?"

Zeke looked across at the youth. He frowned and said, "Don't look for trouble."

"I have to know," Matthew replied.

"It's best you just leave it be. It's best you don't know. And it's best you ride along without me tomorrow."

"You don't have to ride on alone," Matthew said. "There's Indian country up ahead. You'll need the safety of the wagon train same as me."

"I made it this far," Zeke said. He looked at Matthew's face. He could see it was still filled with questions. Zeke sighed. He picked up a stick and played with it. He was trying to decide how and where to begin. "It was an accident," he said finally.

Matthew seemed relieved and almost laughed out loud. "I *knew* it was an accident. I knew you couldn't kill a man on purpose."

"Yeah, well . . . it was an accident, like I said. There are some people back east, they help slaves to escape."

"Who are these people?" Matthew asked.

"People same as you and me. Black and white who think all folks should be free. There are more of them than you might think. But they've got to work in secret, because some states still make it legal to own slaves.

"I was in Missouri," Zeke continued. "They moved me from house to house, mile after mile—mostly at night. I was supposed to meet up with a family who'd take me in for good. But as a *free* man. Then, it happened . . ."

"What happened Zeke? Tell me." Matthew urged him.

"The Harlan brothers. Jeb and Hank. They're like your pa in a way. They hunt— but they hunt for men. They trap and kill them, just like animals. The Harlans found out about the route I took. One night they cornered me in a barn. Hank aimed his gun right at me and fired."

"Did he hit you?"

"The gun backfired. He killed himself, plain and simple. Everyone knew it, too, even Jeb. I ran and hid in an old shack that night. But the next day I heard two men saying that I was the one who killed Hank. The town put a price on my head, and Jeb was coming to get me. I've been on the run ever since. He's no more than a day's ride behind me. So I can't stay with you. If he gets to me there's no telling what he'll do to you."

"I'm not scared," Matthew declared. "Besides, there's two of us Zeke. Harlan doesn't stand a chance. You're strong, and you must have a good aim to bag this hare with one shot. And I'm the sharpest shooter this side of Miller's Ridge."

Matthew's hearty courage almost made Zeke laugh. "If you had any sense, you'd try to take me in yourself."

"Heck," said Matthew. "If I had any sense, I would have stayed in Hatfield's Bluff with my mamma and pa."

Both Zeke and Matthew began to laugh. They laughed long, hard, and loud. It felt good to laugh. A short time later, the two men drifted off to sleep.

It wasn't until dawn that their sleep was interrupted. As an orange glow began to form in the eastern sky, they heard the sound of thunder. It was faint, distant thunder. But it suddenly put fear into their hearts.

Zeke and Matthew looked up to the sky. It was free of clouds, and promised as fine a sunrise as anyone could ask for.

"Can't be a storm on the way," Zeke said.

"Shhh," Matthew said.

"What?"

"Listen."

The two men grew quiet. The thunder grew louder and louder by the moment. Both men realized at the same instant that this was the thunder of animals.

"Buffalo?" Zeke said.

"Too fast, too light," Matthew said. He put his ear to the ground. "Horses," he said. As soon as he said it, they saw a cloud of dust on the horizon.

"Wild horses?" asked Zeke.

"Not enough of them. From the dust, I reckon there's no more than a dozen."

Zeke peered through the gray of the morning. "Riders. I see riders. Indians?"

"Not Indians," Matthew said confidently. "I've seen Indians ride. They don't make that kind of racket. They ride real soft. And they don't stir up the dust like that. Look—"

Both men could just make out the approaching forms. The solid mass began to break up into individual parts. There seemed to be about ten riders. One of them was carrying a red, white, and blue flag. Whoever they were, they were riding as if the very devil was chasing them.

"They're government," Matthew said.

As the group came closer, Matthew could see that they were all in uniform, except for one. He appeared to be an Indian scout. One of the men was strapped face down across his saddle. His horse was tied to the horse of another. Matthew saw that the riders were led by an officer, probably a captain, going by his dress.

In another instant the band of men bore down on Matthew and Zeke. All the horses came to a halt behind the captain. He was a dark man, with a big mustache and long black hair. The dust and dirt could hide neither the fear nor the rage in his eyes. He calmed his horse as best he could and took a swift look behind him.

"Good morning, sir," Matthew said.

"No time for introductions or pleasantries, son," the captain answered. He glanced quickly around the small camp Matthew and Zeke had made. "Looks like there's just the two of you here."

"That's right," Matthew said. "Is anything wrong?"

"As wrong as wrong can be," the captain answered. "You two better come with us. Hit your mounts and ride if you value your lives. We just left an Indian settlement. Seven of my men are back there, face down in the dirt with arrows in their backs."

4

Matthew looked around at the other men. Half of them were bloody and wounded. There were wild looks in their eyes. Even the scout, called Yellow Cloud by the captain, seemed dazed and shaken.

"I won't repeat myself, gentlemen," the captain told Matthew and Zeke. Then he bellowed to his troops, "Hang and rattle, men. Hoaa." The men took off as swiftly as they had arrived.

"Think the Indians will come?" asked Zeke.

"I don't want to find out," Matthew answered. "Let's follow them."

Matthew quickly mounted his horse. But Zeke held back. "What's the matter?" Matthew asked. Zeke just stared at Matthew, a worried look on his face.

"Come on Zeke. You want to wind up like those soliders, with an arrow in your back?"

"I can't go," Zeke said.

It dawned on Matthew why Zeke was so afraid. If the soliders were to learn about Zeke's past, they might arrest him and send him back. But Matthew refused to believe the worst. He figured the soldiers would not be bothered with the problems of the South. They had their own problems—namely the Indians.

"Well, I'm not leaving you here," Matthew said. "As far as they're concerned, you and I set out on our own. You're a ranch hand who worked for my family, all right? Now let's get out of here."

It was a hard six miles to the military camp. At the foot of a hill, Matthew counted about a dozen tents. This was no army. It was just a small garrison of no more than two dozen men.

After they reached camp, Matthew and Zeke settled into a spare tent. They rinsed themselves off with water from a tin pitcher and bowl. Then Zeke sat very still, dog tired from the ride. He stared down at the bare earth beneath him. Matthew knew he was still afraid of being found out. The two men sat in their tent, wondering what would happen next.

Matthew looked over at Zeke. He had his shirt off, a towel draped across his neck. And for the first time, Matthew saw it. On Zeke's left shoulder, barely visible, was a series of small raised bumps. At first Matthew could not figure out what it was. A scar, yes. But from what?

Then he looked more closely. And he saw that the letter "X" had been burned into Zeke's skin. He had been branded, Matthew realized, like a steer. In their brief time together, Matthew had looked upon Zeke as strong and fearless. But now, sitting there, half naked and crouched near the ground, the black man looked different. He seemed small, weak, and full of fear.

Matthew wanted to tell him how sorry he was. He wanted to let Zeke know that he didn't think less of him as a man. He certainly didn't think of Zeke as a "thing" that could be "owned" by another person. If anything, Zeke deserved all the respect in the world for having gone through what he had.

Just as Matthew opened his mouth to speak, the tent flap flew open. Zeke hurriedly threw his shirt over his chest to cover the mark on his shoulder.

"Men?" It was Captain Grade. He had gotten cleaned up and seemed rested now. The fear in his eyes was replaced by a grim determination. "You two men all right?"

"Yes," Matthew said. "Are you?"

The captain was surprised at the question. He showed a slight smile. "Yes, young man, I'll be all right. As soon as I tack a few Indian hides to my tent."

"Just what happened back there?" asked Matthew.

"A while back we made a treaty with the Apaches," the captain said. "Gave them 6600 acres of land around here, far more than they needed. We've had a lot of settlers come out here. But I don't know any good reason why we can't share this land. That's all we want to do, share the land.

"My orders were to resettle some of the savages. Allow for all of us to have a piece of God's earth. But let me tell you, the Apaches have a different idea of fairness, son. You could fit the entire tribe in 600 acres with room to spare. But they want it all. There's a hot-blooded batch of them, about 100, who won't budge."

"Isn't it their land though?" Matthew said innocently. He realized too late that his remark would probably anger the captain. And it did.

"It's *our* land, son. We gave it to them. Hear what I'm saying? Gave them scott-free what it would cost a white man dearly for. *We* aim to *use* this land, do something with it. We want to use it as it was meant to be used. But the savages just sit on it. They're too lazy to do anything but hunt and drink on it."

"So the government wants the land back?" asked Matthew.

"Not really. The aim is to move them to another stretch of land. It's a bit smaller, but just as pretty. And it's just as good for their needs. They wouldn't lose a thing. But you just try telling the Apaches that. They're a thickheaded bunch."

As soon as those words left the captain's lips, he suddenly stared at Matthew. He stared at him long and hard. It was as if he were seeing him for the first time. It dawned on Matthew why. Though Matthew's features were white like his father's, he had his mother's dark, brick-red skin. Usually it was not very noticeable. But now, after weeks under the harsh plains sun, it shone a bright red.

The captain looked both sheepish and a little annoyed at once. "Of course not all Indians are bad, mind you. My Indian scout, Yellow Cloud, is as true and as good a man as they come. I'm not like some. I don't hate just for the sake of hating. But when seven good men get murdered for no earthly reason, I get mad!"

"What are you going to do?" The timid voice came from Zeke, who had remained quiet until then.

"There's no way for a handful of men to roust a hundred Apaches. I sent a rider on ahead to get help. There will be another 100 men here by next week. In the meantime, I don't plan to sit by while the bodies of my men lie rotting on the open plain. Tomorrow we ride back and take an eye for an eye. Just like the Bible says. My men need to get their guts and spirit back. And they will if we take seven Indians to their graves.

"You two are safe here. After the attack we'll ride on to meet the reinforcements.

We can deposit both of you on a wagon train, safe out of Indian country. That's all. There's food in the mess tent. Make yourselves at home."

He walked out, leaving Matthew disturbed and frightened. "He's talking about murder, plain and simple."

"I suppose so," Zeke said. "But what do you call what the Indians did?"

"They're trying to protect what little they got left. My pa told me about these treaties the government signs and then backs out of. Happens all the time. Give the red man some land, then take it away. Till finally there's nothing left. The captain ought to know better."

"Well," said Zeke. "I guess he's got no choice."

"What?"

"He's got a bunch of angry, defeated men on his hands. They want revenge."

"How can *you* of all people say that?" Matthew asked. "How can you just sit there and—"

"Because I know what it feels like to want revenge. I also know that getting angry and upset about it won't change a thing. Those soldiers plan on doing some killing. They're going to do it, with or without our approval. And another thing. I'm not about to say 'boo' to that captain. I've come hundreds of miles to get this far, to be as free as I'll ever be. I won't do *anything* to risk that."

Zeke stormed out of the tent. Matthew suddenly felt alone and out of control. Things were happening too fast. "It just isn't fair," he said to himself. "It's not right to move Indians off one piece of land and put them on another. Not just so whites and Indians can 'share' the land. What gave white people the right to tell the Indians where to live?"

Matthew laid down on his wool blanket and started to doze off. He slept for a few minutes, but was soon awakened by the sound of Zeke's voice. Matthew actually sat up, thinking that Zeke was talking to him. But then he realized that Zeke was still outside the tent. He was talking to someone else. Matthew listened carefully, for he heard fear in Zeke's voice. He soon understood why. Zeke was being addressed by Captain Grade.

"Hello, Zeke. You and the boy have everything you need?"

"Yes sir, we're fine."

"Good. Say, I don't believe you said where you were from."

"Well, uh . . ." Zeke stammered.

"You don't hail from Missouri, do you?"

"Missouri?"

"Yeah. A few days ago I ran into a fella who comes from Missouri," the captain said. "A white man." The captain paused for a moment. Zeke remained silent. Matthew could almost feel the man's fear from the other side of the tent.

"This fella was pretty angry," the captain said. He told me he was looking for someone. He said some Negro fella ran away from his owner and killed this man's brother. Yep, a Negro, that's what he said."

Matthew froze in horror. The captain knew about Zeke! What would he do? Matthew sat inside the tent straining to hear every word.

The captain went on. "Now what do you suppose the odds are of there being two Negroes running around these parts? One being the object of this white man's hunt. And the other just being some innocent wanderer."

"It would be possible, I guess," said Zeke.

"Think so?" the Captain asked. "Maybe you're right. Still, I wonder if both of these Negroes—the innocent and the murderer—would have a brand on them. The kind of brand they give slaves. That would put two Negro slaves right smack in the middle of the same five-mile area." The captain paused a moment before adding. "Now *that* doesn't seem very possible, does it? Now let's see if I can recall this white man's name. Jud? No, ah, Jeb. That's right. Jeb Harlan. Wore a buckskin coat."

"Please sir," said Zeke. "Please . . ."

It was all Matthew could stand. He could no longer sit by while the Captain had his merciless fun with Zeke. He burst out of the tent.

"Now hold on Captain," said Matthew. "Zeke is my pa's ranch hand. Him and me set out together to find our riches, stake a claim. I don't know who's been telling you stories about runaway slaves but—"

Zeke cut Matthew short. "It's no use," he said. "The captain here knows. That man Jeb, he'll be chasing me for the rest of my days. I guess I'd tire sooner or later anyway. No one can keep running forever."

"Better leave this to me, son," said the captain.

"What are you going to do to him?" demanded Matthew. "He hasn't done anything wrong. He didn't kill that man. It was an accident."

The Captain put up his hands in protest to stop Matthew. "Now hold on there, my boy. This has nothing to do with you."

Matthew ignored the captain's warning. "You try to turn this man in . . ." Matthew paused to gather his courage. He knew he was about to say something he would regret. But he could not stop the words. ". . . I'll stop you any way I can!"

"Matthew, shut up," Zeke said.

Matthew tried his best to look fierce. But it wasn't something he was suited for. He was a little put off when he saw a smile come over the captain's face. "I believe you would try to stop me," the captain said. "But I don't think things need to come to that."

Then Captain Grade turned to Zeke. "I don't have any wish to put you in chains," he told him. "As far as this murder goes, I guess you could be just as innocent as you could be guilty. But I'm sworn to uphold the law. Now that man, Jeb, is a day's ride from here. I can either give you to him, or tell him to ride on."

Matthew knew the captain was getting at something. He knew Zeke would be asked to do something in return for Grade's silence.

"I believe a man has to earn his freedom," the captain said. "That's especially true out West. I can promise you freedom. But I need your help with our raid on the Indians."

"Don't do it," Matthew said.

"Hush," Zeke commanded. "Captain? If you can make good on your promise, I'll do whatever you ask."

"What are you saying, Zeke?" Matthew cried.

But Zeke did not answer. He just lowered his head and turned away from Matthew.

The captain, however, looked Matthew right in the eye. "It appears, son, that you have some growing yet to do. If you call this man your friend, you'll get back to your tent and let us talk in private."

Matthew looked on in silence, drowning in his own confusion. He watched Captain Grade lead Zeke away by the shoulder. The two men disappeared into the captain's tent.

CHAPTER
5

Matthew went back into his tent and dropped down onto the wool blanket. He felt lonely and frustrated. He wished he had never left home. He wished he was still helping his father with the furs. Or better yet, he wished his sister had never left home at all. Why couldn't life be just like it was before Hattie left?

It was nearing dusk before Zeke finally came back. Matthew had grabbed some beans and bread from a cranky cook earlier and brought them back to his tent. He was finishing the food when Zeke closed the tent flap behind him.

The big black man said nothing. He sat down across from Matthew and played absently with a twig.

Matthew looked up, held out his plate of food and said, "Want some?"

Zeke said. "No. I ate with the captain."

"I figured you might have," Matthew said quietly. "What did he ask you to do?"

"It's probably best you don't know," said Zeke.

"I want to know."

"He wants me to go with the men on the raid tomorrow night."

"And do what?"

Zeke hesitated. Then he finally said, "The Indians here don't see too many black men. They tend to think black men have magical powers, that they're signs of good fortune. The captain thinks that the Apache leaders would be the most curious. And if I was to appear in their camp as a magic man, well, I could lead them to a nearby creek, then . . ."

Zeke couldn't get the rest of the story out. But Matthew knew what came next. He said ". . . then the captain and his men open fire from behind the rocks and trees and bushes. And they cut down the tribe's leaders just like that. Just like they were hunting buffalo. Just like they were killing a bunch of animals. I swear, Zeke, you did more than eat with the captain. You sold your soul to—"

"Shut up!" cried Zeke. "I've listened to your bellyaching long enough. You moan on and on about the Indians. You don't like it? Then *you do* something about it. You go off and live with them. Fight and die with them, too. But don't talk to me about selling my soul. No sir. I'm getting my soul *back*. That's what I'm doing. I'm gettin' it back!"

He stood and kicked the dirt in anger. Matthew tensed and backed away. Zeke said, "Look around you boy. You can't help but see all sorts of suffering and misery. Black people surely have their share, and so do the Indians. But so do the thousands of white folks who come pouring into the West like locusts. Babies die, cattle die, folks get killed or maybe kill others. It goes on and on all the time. Just cause you finally sit up and take notice doesn't mean it's going to stop. No sir. But I'm gonna do something about it—for me.

"I've had enough misery for a whole tribe of Indians and then some," Zeke went on. "One more day of hell, one more day of shame isn't going to kill me. Tomorrow night I'm going to be free once and for all. When you get an 'X' like the one on my shoulder, then you can preach to me. Till that day, leave me alone! Got that? Now if you don't like it, get out. Go to California and make your fortune. Git!"

Zeke stormed out of the tent. Matthew felt small and childlike. It was as though he had been scolded by his father. Matthew hated himself because he felt like crying. He wanted to show Zeke that he was a real man. He wanted to show he was as bold and as wise as any man. Instead, he felt like a bowl of jelly inside. He felt like some prissy schoolgirl, soft and weak. He heard Zeke's straining words over and over again in his head— "Leave me alone . . . leave me alone."

Matthew finally fell asleep. When he awoke in the middle of the night, he heard Zeke snoring nearby. The man had returned to the tent so quietly that Matthew hadn't heard a sound. Zeke had simply put his head down and slept.

Matthew looked over at the black man. Matthew knew that Zeke must have had just as rough a night as he had. In less than 24 hours, Zeke would lead the captain's soldiers on their raid. The hunted had turned into the hunter.

Matthew realized for the first time that life held no easy answers. It would be a struggle from now on. For himself as well as for Zeke. He hoped that Zeke would be free by tomorrow. He hoped that the white men and the Indians could indeed "share" the land. But whatever happened, Matthew knew that he could not stay another minute in that camp. He could not be a party to the killing that was about to take place.

He would leave tonight. Before dawn. He would leave Zeke and the captain and continue his journey west. He'd head straight for California, to the gold, to seek his fortune. And maybe in a little while, all this would seem like nothing more than a bad dream.

Matthew slept restlessly for the next two hours. Then around four o'clock he got up and dressed quickly. Zeke was sound asleep. Matthew tiptoed over to the entrance of the tent. Then he looked back at the sleeping black man.

"Goodbye, friend," Matthew whispered in a soft voice. He closed the tent flap behind him.

Outside, the night was chilly and unusually damp. Walking softly Matthew found it was easy to sneak past the one sentry. Matthew and Zeke's horses were tied a short distance away from the soldier's mounts. Matthew found his horse quickly. He stroked its head and mane gently to keep him quiet. He placed the saddle carefully on the horse's back.

Then, in one swift motion, he leapt upon the horse, grabbed the reins, and drove his boot deep in the beast's side. He raced out of camp like a tumbleweed in a thunderstorm. Before the sentry knew what had happened, Matthew was already on his way.

Onward he rode into the night, into the west, into the future. And soon he felt nothing but the horse beneath him and the dust in his teeth.

In the dark, he could not see the trail clearly. He could not see the groove of earth dug out by skillful hands. Had he seen the trap, he might have been able to guide his horse over or around it. Instead, Matthew and his horse were suddenly thrown head over hoof. They crashed to the ground in a dusty heap.

The world seemed to be spinning around in a wild circle. Matthew jumped up and reached for his six-shooter. But it was gone. He stumbled around in the dirt, trying to find it. What was going on? Everything seemed to be happening in a feverish dream.

It was the knife that jolted him back to reality. The cold steel pressing into the fleshy part of his neck brought him to his senses.

"Who are you?" a voice growled. "Speak plain or die."

6

Matthew felt a hand grab him by the chin and turn his head. In a flash, he was looking squarely into the eyes of an Indian. He had half expected to see war paint and a headdress of feathers. But instead of bright colors, paint, and beads, Matthew saw a plain face. It was as dark and as hard as a tombstone.

He tried to speak, but the Indian was choking him. Finally the man loosened his grip.

"My name is Matthew Wilder. I mean no harm."

"Did Grade send you?" the Indian asked in a deep, husky voice.

"What?"

"Captain Grade. Did he send you after me?"

"No."

The Indian tightened his grip, a warning to Matthew to speak the truth.

"I swear," said Matthew. "I ran out of the camp tonight."

"Why?"

"I was afraid. I didn't want to be a part of . . ." Matthew stopped short.

"A part of what?" the Indian demanded. He punctuated his sentence with a sharp jab of the knife handle.

"Aghh! Please!" Matthew cried.

"A part of the raid? Is that it?" the Indian asked. Matthew nodded his head once. "I thought so," the Indian said.

He spun Matthew around. Finally, by the light of the moon, Matthew got a better look at the Indian's face. It was Yellow Cloud—Captain Grade's own scout.

"Tell me what you know of the raid, Matthew Wilder."

"What? I can't do that."

"You must tell me. Many lives are at stake."

"Well, lives will be lost either way. Whether I tell you or not. Look. I don't want any part of this. That's why I left. They kill Indians, the Indians kill them. I just want to go to California and find my fortune."

"Your *fortune*, is that it?" Yellow Cloud said harshly. "Come on, my friend. Come with me and I'll show you some people's fortunes."

Matthew began to protest once more. But Yellow Cloud grabbed him by the neck and dragged him to his horse. He tied Matthew's horse to his own, threw Matthew atop his own mount and climbed up in front of him.

They rode through the night that way for several miles. Neither man said a word. Finally they arrived at a creek as dawn was breaking.

Matthew could hear the creek before he could clearly see it. The water babbled and gurgled as it flowed past rocks and fallen tree stumps. With a silver light now visible in the east, Matthew saw shapes taking form. Yellow Cloud's ride had taken them up where the tree line began. Pines reached skyward. Rocks and bluffs peeked out here and there along the jagged horizon.

"There," said Yellow Cloud abruptly. He pointed to some large rocks that sat on the side of the creek bed. It took several minutes before Matthew's eyes adjusted to the light. But when he finally saw it, his blood turned cold. Before him was as strange a sight as he'd ever seen.

Matthew dismounted and walked toward the rocks. There, draped over the stones, were nearly a dozen pieces of clothing. Most of them were women's dresses made from the hides of buffaloes. But there were some smaller pieces too—children's clothing. All the clothes were heavily stained with blood.

Looking closer, Matthew could see that the dresses were ripped and cut. Several were shot through with bullet holes. One dress had no less than a dozen bullet holes in it.

Then he came upon the children's clothing. All were as bloody and manhandled as the adult's clothing. The sight could not have been more sickening to Matthew had the bodies themselves been in the clothes. Matthew turned around to ask Yellow Cloud about the clothes. He nearly jumped when he saw that the Indian was already standing behind him.

Yellow Cloud said, "They were doing their morning chores, washing their clothes, their hair. The children were playing in the creek. They watched the dawn, same as we do now. But it was not the sun they saw come up over the rim of the hill. It was some of Grade's men. The women and children were no more than targets for the soldiers. This was the 'fortune' of the women and children at Crow Creek. No gold, no silver, just a few moments of terror. Then the horrible silence of death."

Yellow Cloud knelt and touched the hem of one of the small dresses. "We leave the clothing to stain the rocks to remind the spirits of what happened here."

Matthew walked away, unable to take in the sight before him for another moment. Yellow Cloud rose and followed.

"So that's why the Apaches attacked Grade and his men," Matthew said. "In revenge for the murder of the Apache women and children."

"After the raid the soldiers were tired from their morning kill," Yellow Cloud said. Yellow Cloud, but what good will it do? Maybe the best thing for the Apaches to do is to let the white man share the land. It would end the killing, the hatred."

Yellow Cloud knelt and picked up a handful of dirt. "Is that what Grade told you? He just wants to 'share' the land?" He laughed harshly.

"I was raised by a white woman," Yellow Cloud went on. "I went to your schools from the time I was a young man. I studied hard. For a time I hated the Indian more than the white man. I wanted to be a doctor. To be a rich man. But since I could speak English as well as my native tongue, I was sent out here. To help resettle the Indian. Take him off his soil.

"Look at this soil. A hundred miles west of here, there is soil much like this. And beneath it there is gold. As near as the government can make out, there is a wealth of it. And it will do for this territory what the gold has done for the white man in California. In five years time there may be a thousand people standing where we are right now. Rich men, most of them. And they may never be aware that their good fortunes were found at the expense of the Indian."

"But it doesn't have to be like that. In California—"

"In California the Chumash and the Gabrieleno Indians populated the shores. They stood atop the soil where the gold lay buried. But when the white man came and found the gold, he pushed the Indian back further and further. Many that left died, and those who would not leave were killed. The government made treaties. But whenever they found something they wanted on the land, they broke their promises. Just as they are doing here."

It was hard for Matthew to hear the truth. But Yellow Cloud continued to tell his story. "People said that the gold in California ran like rivers. But the blood also ran like rivers. The blood of my people . . . *your* people, my brother."

What a strange expression. Matthew had never heard an Indian call him "brother." He knew he was part-Indian, but he had always felt like a white man. Always thought of himself as a white man.

As Matthew listened to Yellow Cloud, he felt strangely lost and found at the same time. Suddenly his drive to bathe himself in gold seemed to fall away. And for the first time in his whole life, he felt a true kinship with an Indian. Not admiration, but something rooted deep in his soul. This feeling made him calm and peaceful.

At the same time he felt as though he could not completely cut off his white heritage. The fact remained that he was both a white man and a red man. And that made him feel lost and alone.

Zeke had made *his* decision. Now Matthew would have to make his. Yellow Cloud was forcing him to make a choice. And no matter what choice he made, he'd be betraying a part of his heritage. Matthew was learning just how unfair life could be.

Finally he looked up at Yellow Cloud and said, "I'll tell you. I'll tell you about the raid. But we've got to warn Zeke."

"There is no time for that now," Yellow Cloud said. "We will have to put it into the hands of the Spirit. And you and I will have to do our best to see that no harm comes to your friend."

At dusk later that day, Matthew and Yellow Cloud waited and watched. Then they caught their first glimpse of Zeke marching the Apache leaders toward a small grove of trees. Matthew's heart began to pound. Everything was still working according to Grade's plan. Zeke appeared to be stiff and nervous. But he did not have to be very convincing as a magic man. Thanks to Matthew, the Apaches were well prepared for his arrival.

Because Matthew knew of the plan, he could spot where Grade and his men were lying in wait. Matthew thought it was almost funny how obvious the soldiers were. By contrast, the Apaches seemed to be nowhere in sight. It was as though they were invisible. From where he was,

Matthew could see Captain Grade quite clearly. And almost as soon as Matthew spied the captain, he saw another man crouching beside him. Matthew had never seen this man before. But he was sure he knew who he was.

The man was not one of Grade's men. He was not in uniform. In the failing light, Matthew could just make out a fringed buckskin jacket. He knew it was the same buckskin jacket he had heard Captain Grade mention.

Matthew froze in terror. Captain Grade was kneeling beside Jeb Harlan. The bounty hunter who had been chasing Zeke all the way from Missouri was right here!

Matthew uttered a muffled curse. He realized now that the captain had never intended to let Zeke go free. He was just using him. After the raid, he would hand Zeke over to Harlan. And no doubt get part of the reward money, Matthew thought.

All was quiet except for the wind rushing through the trees. Now and then a few angry crows squabbled and snapped at one another. Crickets, anxious for the night, began to chirp. But the men in the grove made no sound.

A snapping twig was the only warning the Apaches gave. And suddenly, the grove was filled with whoops, hollers, and war cries. The Indians dropped from the trees, and sprang from the bluffs and bushes.

Arrows and gunshots quickly filled the air. As planned, two warriors on horseback swooped down on Zeke. Then they quickly dragged him through the river and away from the fight.

Matthew saw Jeb Harlan emerge from the woods and aim his rifle at Zeke. He had a clear shot. But just then a loud gunshot rang through the trees on the bluff. Matthew's gun was still smoking when Yellow Cloud looked down and saw Harlan fall to his knees. Then both men watched him slump over—dead. Matthew closed his eyes and muttered a prayer. He felt sick to his stomach.

The other soldiers, seeing that they were outnumbered quickly began to retreat. But Captain Grade held his ground. "Stand and fight!" he cried bitterly to his men. "Stand and fight!"

He raised his gun and fired twice as the Indians advanced. Those two shots brought down two Apache warriors. But those were the last two shots the captain ever fired. As he reloaded his revolver, a dozen arrows found their way into Grade's chest. The captain screamed in pain and then fell backward over a tree stump.

Matthew turned away. But he could still hear the fading cries of the Indians as they ran after the retreating soldiers. Most of the soldiers rode off to safety. But four others, besides Harlan and Captain Grade, lay on the grassy carpet of the grove. Nearby lay the bodies of the two Indians Grade had killed.

Matthew stood atop the bluff and looked down at Zeke. They seemed to notice each other at the same moment. Matthew waved. A dazed but grateful Zeke waved back. But Matthew could see that Zeke was more interested in the man in the fringed buckskin jacket who lay in silence near a large rock.

Matthew watched as Zeke rolled Harlan over to make sure he was dead. Zeke could not seem to believe his eyes. Matthew thought he heard him say, "It's all over. My God, it's all over."

The soldiers had all seen Zeke carried away. They would assume he was killed by the Indians. Harlan and Grade were both dead. Zeke was free now.

But Matthew knew it was far from over. It would not be over for the Apaches. More soldiers would arrive. And the fighting would continue. More men, red and white, would lose their lives. And if Yellow Cloud was right, the White Man would eventually win. The Indians would have to give up this land and move to a new place. Then even *that* land would be taken from them.

And what of Matthew and Yellow Cloud? Matthew was sure that the soldiers would soon realize they had been betrayed. The soldiers knew that both men had vanished from camp on the same day. They would know that both of them helped the Apaches plan their attack. Matthew Wilder and Yellow Cloud would be hunted men for a long, long time.

Night soon fell. Matthew found himself staring at the same moon and stars he had pondered a week ago. Yet they were not the same. For those stars were the stars a young man makes wishes on. And that moon was the one a young man sings to, drunk on its rays. But tonight, for Matthew Wilder, the stars were nothing more than lights in the sky. And the moon was just something that shines on the coyotes to make them howl.

A Question of Freedom

Lucy Jane Bledsoe

1

Elizabeth's long black hair flew behind her. Beads of sweat ran down her face. She had on her best dress, the red one that Daryl had given her years ago when they were first married. Now its long skirts dragged in the mud as she ran through the woods. Her sleeves kept tearing on tree branches. She gulped for air and tried to run faster.

"Daryl!" Elizabeth screamed, and tripped. She fell to the ground on her hands and knees. She bent over, grabbing her stomach. She could run no more.

But then she heard dogs growling. She also heard the sound of boots pounding through the woods. The sound was getting closer. She had to keep moving and find the river.

Elizabeth struggled to her feet and began to run again. The forest was pitch black. Her heavy dress slowed her down. She fell once again, tripping over a log. She lay in the soft, wet leaves for a moment. But at the sound of barking dogs she dragged herself up again.

Her heart racing with fear, Elizabeth screamed her husband's name again. She jumped over rocks and dodged trees. Finally she saw the muddy water of the McCall River.

Elizabeth's heart now seemed to stop and sink to the bottom of her stomach. She remembered she couldn't swim.

She dove in anyway. Then she heard the first gunshot. Then another. Her legs and arms felt heavy. She was going to drown. She kicked and splashed in the water, gasping for air. Men were shouting at her from the bank of the river. She began to go under. A hand grabbed her. Elizabeth screamed.

"Wake up. Elizabeth! It's me, Daryl. You're having a bad dream. Wake up, Elizabeth. It's all right now."

"Oh, Daryl." Elizabeth let her husband hold her. She was bathed in sweat. So were the sheets on her bed.

"I heard you screaming," Daryl said. "It's all right now, dear. What were you dreaming about?"

Elizabeth was still shaking. Her heart was pounding so hard she thought it would come out of her chest. "I'll be all right now," she was finally able to say. "Let me get up and wash."

"Why don't you just stay in bed a while. You need some rest."

"No, I'll get up. Please, Daryl."

Daryl stood up. He knew that set look on his wife's face. It meant she could not be reasoned with now. He left her alone.

Elizabeth fell back onto her feather pillows and breathed deeply. She wished she could tell Daryl about her dream. She wanted so much to tell him everything. But she needed a few minutes alone to think, to decide what to do.

The dream had to do with what she had heard least night, of course. Yet she couldn't possibly tell Daryl where she had been. Never in a hundred years.

"Oh, what have I done?" Elizabeth moaned out loud. She had never lied to her husband before. Ever! How could she be so foolish. Daryl would see the lie all over her face. He often knew when something was wrong, almost before she did.

Elizabeth decided she would just have to put last night out of her mind. She would pretend it never happened.

And she would never do such a thing again. Then it wouldn't really be a lie. It would just be a mistake. And it would be finished.

As Elizabeth brushed her long dark hair, her hands were shaking. She would never be able to forget what she'd learned last night. She felt like she had been changed forever. She felt like a part of herself was being called forward, and she couldn't hold back. Even if it meant the ruin of everything she had lived for up until now— her home, Daryl, and her whole way of life.

Elizabeth knotted her hair at the back of her neck and put on a blue dress. She quietly went downstairs to join Daryl for breakfast.

At the table Daryl was reading the *Maryland Gazette*. Elizabeth picked up part of the newspaper. Everything in the paper reminded her of last night's meeting: Abraham Lincoln, slavery, and war between the states. The Maryland Gazette believed Lincoln might be elected president of the United States. If he were elected, there would surely be a war between the North and the South. Several Southern states were already threatening to leave the Union.

Elizabeth put her head in her hands. All she and Daryl wanted was to live on their farm in peace. But war would surely destroy their lives.

Elizabeth and Daryl Stellar had been married for ten years. Elizabeth could not imagine being any happier. She loved Daryl more than anyone in the world. He was playful, kind, and a wonderful talker. Besides that, he had always respected Elizabeth's choice of friends and activities.

Daryl made a good living as a businessman. They lived on a small farm just outside of Baltimore, Maryland. They bought it shortly after they were married, and planned on spending the rest of their lives there.

More than anything else about the farm, Elizabeth loved the garden. Her cousin Martha thought it wasn't ladylike for a woman of her position to dig around in the dirt. But Elizabeth wouldn't let anyone else touch her garden. She loved nothing more than to spend hours planting her favorite flowers.

Elizabeth had always believed that nothing could ever spoil her and Daryl's perfect happiness.

However, dark clouds had been gathering over the South for several years. Now, in 1860, it looked as if the dark clouds might burst. The whole country was being torn apart over the question of slavery. Talk of war was everywhere. Elizabeth and Daryl had said to each other that they would stay out of it. They would let others fight the fights.

After last night, though, Elizabeth was beginning to realize that might not be possible.

Corinn, the Stellars' only servant, set a bowl of fresh fruit and cream in front of Elizabeth. She drank her coffee slowly, but couldn't touch the food.

"I should tell Daryl right now," Elizabeth thought. "Before it becomes a real lie. He will be angry. But I won't ever go there again. It will be over with."

Suddenly Daryl dropped the newspaper and scowled. He began to eat his strawberries.

"Now," Elizabeth said to herself. "Tell him right now."

"Elizabeth."

"Yes?" she said, a little startled when Daryl spoke her name.

"What's the matter?" he asked.

"Oh, nothing. I guess I'm a little nervous because I didn't sleep well."

"Yes, you do look tired. I'm sorry you had a bad night."

"Now is your chance," Elizabeth thought. "Out with it."

"Well, anyway," Daryl went on, "I thought you told me you were going to see Ann last night."

Elizabeth's heart skipped a beat. She had been caught.

"Well, uh . . . yes, I did go to see her."

"I stopped by there on the way home from my meeting. I thought I would walk you home. No one was there."

"Oh, of course not." Elizabeth swallowed hard. Was this all he knew? Only that she wasn't at Ann's? She forgot about telling the truth. "We went out for a walk."

"Two women alone?"

"We didn't go far. And really, it wasn't dark yet at 8:30."

"Well, nearly. I don't approve of ladies walking alone at night. Even if some people do."

"Oh, Daryl," Elizabeth smiled, and Daryl smiled back at her. They had a good understanding in their marriage. They both believed that each should have the freedom to grow and explore new ideas and friends. Lying, however, was not part of their understanding.

"All right," Daryl said, still smiling. "I suppose that freethinking friend of yours, Ann, is putting more new ideas in your head. Next thing I know, you'll be wearing bloomers."

"Well," Elizabeth said, putting her chin up in the air. "As a matter of fact, I wanted to try on a pair. Don't you think they would be perfect for gardening?"

Daryl just shook his head and laughed a little. He folded the paper and pushed across the table to Elizabeth. "I've got to get to work early. It's been very busy at the office."

"Will you be home for dinner?"

"I'm not sure."

"Honey, you're working too hard."

"Don't worry, Elizabeth, I'm fine." He kissed her and left the house.

Elizabeth leaned back in her chair and let out a long breath. She was filled with relief. Daryl didn't know where she'd gone last night. And she hadn't really lied to him. She *had* gone to see Ann and they *had* gone for a walk. She'd just left out the part about *where* they'd gone.

Elizabeth's good friend, Ann Williams, had taken her to an abolitionist meeting. The abolitionists were the people working to end slavery in the South. They had helped more than 50,000 slaves escape north to freedom on the "underground railroad." That was the name people had given to the swift and secret way the runaway slaves escaped—even though no one ever went underground or rode a railroad. Helping slaves escape was dangerous work, and it was against the law.

Elizabeth had listened closely at the meeting, and had become deeply disturbed. The idea of people *owning* other people was wrong. Elizabeth had always known that in her heart. And the idea of people *hunting* runaway slaves was terrible. Of course, that was where her bad dream had come from. The speaker at last night's meeting had also read part of the Constitution. It said, "All men are created equal. . . ." He said that meant black people, too.

A part of Elizabeth believed every single word the man said. Even so, white and black people in the South had lived like this for years. It was the normal way of life, the only way of life Elizabeth had ever known. Why were the abolitionists trying to change everything now? Why were they forcing the country into a war between the North and the South?

Elizabeth knew she had no business even thinking about this question. Daryl's whole job depended on slavery. His company exported products from the South. These were farm products that slaves harvested from the fields. Imagine what he would say if he knew his wife had gone to an abolitionist meeting!

"He will never know," Elizabeth said to herself. "I will not even think about these things anymore."

"May I take your breakfast dishes?"

Elizabeth jumped and swung around. "Oh, Corinn. I didn't know you were in the room. You frightened me."

"I'm sorry, ma'am."

"Yes, I'm finished with breakfast," Elizabeth said. Then she added, though she never had before, "Thank you."

Elizabeth was glad that she and Daryl had only one slave. Besides, Elizabeth hardly thought of Corinn as a slave, anyway. Corinn had been in the family for as long as Elizabeth could remember. Corinn and Elizabeth had been born in the same year. The girls played together when they were children. When they grew older, they were kept apart. That was how things were in the South.

When Elizabeth married Daryl, her father sent Corinn to live with them. Elizabeth was delighted.

Elizabeth knew that Corinn was a serious and quiet woman who would never cause trouble. Elizabeth was certain that Corinn was as happy in their home as she and Daryl were.

2

That afternoon Elizabeth's reading club was going to meet at her house. Ann Williams, Elizabeth's cousin, Martha Murphy, and their friend Priscilla Thompson were in the group. The four women used to have a pleasant time reading, talking, and sewing. But lately all they seemed to do was argue. It all started a year ago when they read that best-seller, *Uncle Tom's Cabin*. It was written by an abolitionist named Harriet Beecher Stowe. The ideas in the book caused the women to think a lot about the issue of slavery. And it had caused some hard feelings.

"Corinn," Elizabeth called on her way to the kitchen. "We'll only need coffee this afternoon. I think I'll make my cinnamon rolls."

"I can make the rolls, ma'am." Corinn said.

Elizabeth was surprised. She always made the cinnamon rolls. She used an old family recipe. "That's all right, Corinn. I'm looking forward to making them," she said.

Corinn glanced at the pantry. "What do you need from the panty? Flour and what else? I'll get it."

"Really, Corinn. Don't you have the dusting and cleaning to do? I'll take care of this."

Elizabeth had a puzzled look on her face as she watched Corinn leave the room. It was unlike Corinn to not know just what was expected of her.

Elizabeth shrugged and went to the kitchen. Her cousin Martha also thought the kitchen was no place for a lady. Elizabeth laughed a little thinking of Martha. The two women had grown up on neighboring farms. They had been best friends since they could walk. They had spent hours riding horses and climbing trees with their brothers and the slave children.

The difference between Martha and Elizabeth was that Martha had outgrown the children's games. Elizabeth had never outgrown adventure. That was something that Martha couldn't accept. She had always taken it upon herself to let Elizabeth know how she should act. Elizabeth usually just laughed it off.

Lately, the differences between the two of them had become a bit more serious. But Martha was family. Elizabeth did her best to ignore their differences.

Elizabeth carried two bowls to the pantry. She filled one with raisins. The other bowl was for the flour. But when she took the top off the flour barrel, she saw that it was nearly empty. How strange, she thought. She was sure she had bought a barrel not long ago. She looked in the cornmeal barrel, and it, too, was low. She supposed she and Daryl had been eating at home a lot more often lately.

Just as she was finishing the cinnamon rolls, there was a knock at the kitchen door. Elizabeth knew what Martha would say about the lady of the house answering the kitchen door! But Corinn was upstairs dusting. Elizabeth pulled open the door.

A tall, good-looking black man stood with a bunch of flowers in his hand. She recognized him as Jonathan, a slave on a farm outside of town.

Jonathan looked startled when he saw Elizabeth. He certainly had not expected *her* to answer the door.

"I'm sorry, ma'am. I, well—"

"Are you delivering something?" Elizabeth asked.

"No, ma'am," Jonathan said, holding his flowers tightly. The two stood staring at each other, not knowing what to do. It was clear to Elizabeth that Jonathan had been sent to town to do something for his master. He had taken the opportunity to stop and give these flowers to Corinn. She also knew that this side trip would be cause for punishment if his master found out about it.

Elizabeth remembered seeing Corinn talking with Jonathan in town once or twice before. She had wondered then if there were something between them. But she had never asked Corinn about it. Maybe she should have.

Elizabeth now looked at the tall man before her, and tried to decide what to do next. She was supposed to act angry. She should tell him she did not want to see him on their property again. But Elizabeth simply couldn't. She was touched by the flowers. She wanted Corinn to have them.

She tried to cover up her softer feelings by speaking sternly. She said, "I suppose those are for Corinn."

"Well, yes, ma'am."

"Give them to me. I'll see that she gets them."

Jonathan became nervous. His hands were shaking and he began to step backward. "Well, thank you, ma'am, but I don't . . ." Elizabeth reached for the flowers.

Jonathan yanked the flowers back. He moved so fast the whole bunch slipped in his hand and loosened. A piece of paper went fluttering from the center of the flowers to the ground.

Jonathan jumped after the paper like it was a hundred-dollar bill. Then he turned and left quickly, taking his note and flowers, without saying another word.

Elizabeth shut the kitchen door slowly. She had a feeling that something odd was going on. There were plenty of reasons Jonathan might have been frightened. He could have thought Elizabeth would tell his master he had come here. Or, that she would read the note. Or even punish Corinn. Even so, there was something more in Jonathan's face. It was something Elizabeth could not quite put her finger on.

She decided not to mention Jonathan's visit, either to Corinn or to Daryl. She continued to get ready for her reading group.

3

Everything was ready by the time the first guest arrived. Elizabeth hoped the knock at the door was Ann. But when Corinn showed the guest into the drawing room, it was Priscilla. Priscilla wore a fancy, full dress that was covered with flowers. "She always overdresses," thought Elizabeth.

"Wasn't the meeting last night exciting!" Priscilla squealed right away. "I thought the speaker was so good-looking, didn't you? Too bad he's a minister!" Priscilla giggled and took off her gloves.

"Priscilla!" Elizabeth said glancing nervously at Corinn.

"Oh!" Priscilla slapped a hand over her mouth. "I should learn to be more careful."

"Things are getting bad," Elizabeth thought, "if I have to hide my activities from Corinn."

When Corinn had left the room, Elizabeth said, "I didn't mean to snap at you, Priscilla. But you know the abolitionist meetings are . . . well, it's dangerous to be there. Even the public ones like last night. Please don't mention to anyone else that I was there. I will not be going to another meeting."

"You won't? But how can you stay away from that good-looking minister? Those blue eyes are too much for me!" Priscilla put two cinnamon rolls on a plate. "These look *sooo* good."

Elizabeth was relieved when the bell rang again and Ann came in. Next to Daryl, Ann was her favorite person in the world. She was wearing a simple blue dress and had a serious look on her face.

"Well, have you thought it over?" Ann asked her two friends right away. "Do you think you will be able to do some work for us?"

"You can count on me," Priscilla said. Then she giggled. "As long as that minister is part of the group."

"Elizabeth?" Ann took her friend's hand.

"Ann, I admire the work you are doing so much. But you know Daryl's business is all tied up with slavery. How could I? I'm sorry. I've already gone too far."

Ann stepped back. She looked disappointed. "All right. But I want to warn you about one thing. I don't think we should talk about this in front of Martha anymore."

"Why not?" Priscilla asked.

"I know she doesn't hold our—well, *my*—point of view," Ann said. "And it's just not safe anymore with—"

Ann cut herself off in midsentence when she noticed Corinn. She had come in silently with a fresh pot of coffee and was standing in a corner waiting to pour it.

"We still have plenty of coffee," Elizabeth said to her. Just then the bell rang, and Corinn left to answer it.

Martha burst into the room. "Well! The worst has happened," she nearly shouted. Her face was red with anger.

"What?" asked Elizabeth.

"Three of our slaves ran away last night!" Martha said. She threw an angry look toward Corinn.

"Oh, my gosh," Priscilla said in a high-pitched voice.

Elizabeth remained silent. She looked around at her friends. Priscilla was on the edge of her chair. Ann was studying her nails. Martha was throwing her hat and coat on a chair.

"We have $1000 out on each of the men, and $700 on the woman," Martha said. "I am so angry. And people like you, Ann, are encouraging it." She pointed a finger.

"You know how I feel, Martha," Ann said. "There's no use getting into it."

"No use getting into it! Did you hear that, Elizabeth?" Martha yanked off her gloves. She always tried to get Elizabeth to take her side. "I think you'd feel different if you lost thousands of dollars worth of property."

"You haven't," Ann said quietly.

"Haven't what?" Priscilla asked.

"It is impossible for a human being to be the property of someone else," Ann said. "You talk as if you can put a price tag on someone's head. As if a person were a cow or a horse!"

"I don't know how far you've gone with those abolitionists," Martha said, her voice deep and shaking. But there was a time when you had more sense. For your own good, I would like to remind you of the law. You can be fined a good deal of money—and even thrown into jail—for helping runaway slaves."

"Thank you for informing me of the law," Ann said hotly.

"You know," Martha said, shaking her finger at Ann. "You think you are so above us all. But think about the facts. A slave has harvested most of the food you eat. A slave has picked the cotton that your fine dresses are made from. That's the way this country works."

"Oh, please," Elizabeth said. "Let's get to talking about this week's book. There is no need for arguing. Martha, I'm sorry about . . ."

Both Martha and Ann eyed her sharply. She knew that each expected her to take their own side. Elizabeth never finished her sentence.

A few nights later, Elizabeth and Daryl were enjoying a quiet evening at home. Daryl's work had been keeping him at the office late almost every night. Elizabeth was happy to have him at home early for once.

After dinner, they settled in the drawing room with coffee. Daryl was his old self, telling her funny stories about people in his office. These were Elizabeth's favorite times. She had just begun telling Daryl her new plans for the back garden. Suddenly, there was a loud banging on the door.

"I'll get it," Daryl said. Elizabeth followed him to the door.

"Hello!" called Brian Murphy, Martha's husband. He was a thick man with small brown eyes. Elizabeth looked from his face down to his hands. Her eyes locked on the long, shiny barrel of a gun.

"Good evening," Daryl said. It was then that Elizabeth saw the shapes of several men standing in the dark behind Brian. As her eyes got used to the dark, she saw that they all had guns. One man had two dogs on a leash.

"Listen, we're putting together a committee," Brian Murphy said. "You probably heard we lost three slaves a few days ago. The Smiths lost five last night." Brian jerked his thumb at Lane Smith, the man holding the dogs. "Seems as if the underground railroad goes right through here. Runaway slaves have been

passing through right under our noses."
His eyes narrowed.

"What do you want from us?" Elizabeth
stepped up next to Daryl.

"We're out to catch the slaves or the
folks helping them. Either way, there's big
reward money." Brian smiled.

"It's time we took this matter into our
own hands," Smith added. "Its time to fight
back."

"We thought you might want to help
out," Brian Murphy said.

"I'm sorry, but this had nothing to do
with us. We can't help you," Daryl said.
He started to close the door. Brian put
his big boot in the way.

"Yes?" Daryl asked.

"Do you know who Harriet Tubman is?"

"Yes, we've read about her. She's the
runaway slave that has been helping a lot
of other slaves escape."

"That's right. And do you know what
the price is on her head?"

Elizabeth thought of what Ann would
say. How can you put a price tag on the
head of a human being?

"Look—" Daryl began, trying to shut the
door again. He didn't care if Brian Murphy
was family. He wasn't going to have a

group of gun-carrying men on his doorstep.

But Brian's foot was still in the door. "Forty thousand dollars. That's how much. And that's how serious this is getting. You may think you can stay out of it. But no one can anymore. Everyone has to take sides. If Lincoln gets elected later this year, there's sure to be war. I know where I'll be. Where are you going to stand, Stellar?"

"Look, I'm not interested in running around looking for slaves with guns and dogs," Daryl said. "You think we're keeping runaways here? You want to look through my house? Go ahead. Just leave your guns and dogs outside."

"And your dirty boots," Elizabeth added, her voice cracking with anger.

Brian looked back at the men with him. Smith shrugged. Brian shrugged, too. "No," he said. "We don't think you're hiding runaways here. But keep your ears open. There's big money for any leads that help with the capture of runaways. How about that girl of yours. What's her name? Corinn. She may be in on something."

"Corinn?" Daryl laughed softly. "It's not possible."

"Never." Elizabeth backed him up.

"Don't be too sure," Brian said. "You may want to question her. Let her know you know what's been going on around here. Well, good night. Sorry to have disturbed your evening."

"They're going too far," Daryl said after shutting the door. "Hunting people for a reward! What are people coming to today?"

Elizabeth agreed. But if that were going too far, where did it stop? What part of slavery was *not* going to far, she wondered.

Brian Murphy was right about one thing. Sooner or later, everyone had to take sides. It looked more and more like a war was coming between the North and South. Elizabeth did not want to have to take sides. But after all, they *were* Southerners. They were even slave owners.

Elizabeth's evening with Daryl had been ruined. After the men left, Daryl slipped into complete silence. Lately, he had been strangely distant and quiet much of the time. Elizabeth wondered if he still loved her as much as he used to. He hardly ever told her what was on his mind anymore.

Elizabeth lay awake in bed that night. She was afraid to sleep for fear of having more bad dreams. She could not stop thinking about the dogs and shiny barrels of the guns. Worst of all, though, was the look on Brian's face. He looked almost as if he were playing a game he enjoyed.

Elizabeth lay awake for a long time listening to the silent night. Then, at about three in the morning, she thought she heard something. She sat up in bed to listen more carefully.

There it was again. Footsteps downstairs.

It must be Daryl, she decided. He probably couldn't sleep, either. Perhaps he got up to make himself a sandwich. Elizabeth got out of bed. She thought she'd make a cup of tea and keep Daryl company.

Elizabeth walked quietly out of her bedroom into the hall. The door to Daryl's bedroom was open. She tiptoed up to it. Daryl made a small mountain in the middle of the bed. He was breathing as softly as a baby.

Elizabeth froze. Then who was downstairs? She started to wake Daryl, but then stopped herself. She was probably just imagining the footsteps. After all, she had been imagining all kinds of crazy things lately.

Of course, it was all in her head. She had been worrying too much. She would go downstairs right now. A cup of tea would calm her. And she would prove to herself, once and for all, that she was just imagining things.

Elizabeth crept down the stairs, one step at a time. Her insides felt as if they were made of jelly.

At the kitchen door, she stopped. Someone *was* there. She heard him plainly now. Elizabeth took a deep breath and threw open the kitchen door.

"Corinn!" Elizabeth could not believe her eyes. Corinn was fully dressed, and had several apples in her apron. "What in the world are you doing?"

Corinn looked as calm as ever. Her eyes were steady and clear. She said, "I was worried, ma'am. I started to think I had left the top off the sugar barrel. You know how bad the ants can be. I thought it would be terrible if they got in the sugar."

"You got up in the middle of the night to see if you put the top on the sugar barrel?"

"Yes, ma'am."

"But what are you doing with all those apples?"

"I'm sorry. I got hungry."

Elizabeth stared at Corinn. She knew this was a lie. And she knew that Corinn knew she knew. The apples were for someone else. Too many thoughts were crowding Elizabeth's head at once. She pushed them away. She didn't want to know. Softly, she said, "Corinn, you had better be careful."

Then Elizabeth turned around and left the kitchen.

4

The next morning Elizabeth put on a hat and her new bloomers. She was going to put five new rose plants in the backyard. She hoped that would take her mind off the strange things that were happening.

The day was clear and blue, perfect for gardening. But as she entered the garden, she stopped short. She heard a noise near the small garden cottage where Corinn lived.

"That's funny," she thought. She had sent Corinn to town a few minutes ago. Elizabeth looked around slowly. Then, feeling braver than last night, she walked quietly toward the cottage.

She saw the back of a woman crouched at one of the windows. The woman's hands were cupped around her face as she looked in.

"Hello?" Elizabeth called to the woman's back.

"What!" the woman cried, jumping up. "Oh! Elizabeth . . . I was . . ."

"Martha!" Elizabeth stepped closer. "Whatever are you doing?"

Martha brushed off her dress and patted her hair. Then she put on a smile. "How silly of me. I know you had been talking about doing something special to the back garden. And since I was out on a walk, I came to see what you had done. I would have come to the door if it weren't so early. I'm sorry. Did I frighten you?"

"No," Elizabeth said. "But why are you looking in Corinn's cottage?"

"This is Corinn's room?" Martha's face was all innocence. "I thought it was your garden room. It's such a cute house for a servant. Why did you ever give her such lovely quarters?"

Martha was quick. Elizabeth decided not to ask any more questions. It would do no good. Besides, she wasn't hiding any runaways, so what difference did it make? Let Martha sniff around all she wanted.

"As for the flower beds," Elizabeth said. "I'm just beginning them this morning."

"You really should get a man to do your gardening. It's terrible on your hands. Daryl is certainly able to pay someone."

"I like to do it," Elizabeth said. She turned her back to Martha and picked up the shovel.

"My goodness, what have you got around your legs, Elizabeth!"

"Bloomers," Elizabeth said coldly.

"Well!" Martha waited for Elizabeth to say more. When she didn't, Martha said, "I'll see you at the reading club next week, then. Remember, it's at my house."

This time Martha left through the front of the house. On her way out, she passed Ann, who was coming in.

Ann said to Elizabeth, "I didn't know you were having company this morning."

"I didn't either," Elizabeth answered. She pushed the shovel in the ground with extra force.

"Are you okay?" Ann asked.

"Yes, I'm fine, thank you." Elizabeth leaned the shovel against the house. She calmed down and smiled at Ann.

"I came to tell you something really exciting," Ann said. "Frederick Douglass is speaking in town! Can you believe it? He'll be there this afternoon. You must come with me. This is something not to miss."

"I can't," Elizabeth said. "You know that. I can't risk being seen in a crowd of abolitionists again. It might ruin Daryl's job." Elizabeth spoke the words as if they were forced on her. She wanted to go, very much. But she had to stay out of it. Her husband's job was not the only thing at risk. Her marriage was also at risk. That was too much to risk giving up.

"No," Elizabeth said out loud, more to herself than to Ann. "I simply can't."

"I'm trying to understand," Ann said. "I know how hard this must be for you."

"Thank you," Elizabeth said. "I wish . . . I wish it were different."

When Daryl came home for lunch he looked as if his mind were elsewhere. Elizabeth told him about the roses she had planted. He didn't even smile.

"I'm afraid I won't be home this evening, Elizabeth," he said as he finished eating. "I have to take the two o'clock train to Washington. My meeting will run too late to get back home tonight."

Elizabeth kept herself from saying, "Again?" She was tired of Daryl being away from home so much.

When Daryl left the house, Elizabeth went upstairs. She sat in her room thinking about how much Daryl had changed in the past few months. He used to be so full of fun all the time. That was what she loved most about him. Lately, he had become so serious. He looked as if he were always troubled by something.

Of course, Elizabeth told herself, it was the upcoming election. That was on everyone's mind. If Lincoln was elected, if there were war, Daryl's business could be ruined.

"It's not me," Elizabeth said out loud. "He's being so quiet because of *other* troubles." She wanted to believe that. Even so, it was not like Daryl to not talk with her about his problems. Elizabeth stood and walked the length of the room. She turned and walked back. She felt restless. Her thoughts turned to Ann going to hear Frederick Douglass speak. Then she pictured her husband safely on the train to Washington.

Suddenly, Elizabeth ran downstairs. She put on her hat and coat. Next thing she knew, she was out the door.

She hurried along the streets of Baltimore, looking around nervously. She nodded to people she knew. Did they know where she was going? Perhaps they would mention to Daryl that they had seen her. Even worse, maybe Martha was following her. She did not know whom she could trust anymore.

She got to the church just as Frederick Douglass took the speaker's stand. Ann spied her right away and a big smile came across her face. Elizabeth worked her way through the crowd to Ann's side. Her friend hugged her.

Frederick Douglass spoke about how he had run away to his own freedom. He spoke beautifully, and Elizabeth was deeply moved.

Yet even as she listened, she remembered the committee of angry men at their door a few nights ago. She remembered reading about newspaper writers who had been tarred and feathered for writing abolitionist stories. Perhaps there was a price on her very own head— just for being at this meeting!

At the same time, she thought of Daryl in Washington. She had gone with him once into that city. She shivered just remembering it. Washington had the biggest slave market in the country. Right before her eyes people had been made to stand up on blocks. Slave owners yelled out prices, as if these people were cattle. Brokenhearted children were sold away from their mothers and fathers. Elizabeth had seen nothing like it before. She had told Daryl she would never go with him to Washington again.

"I appear before you," Douglass was saying, "as a thief and a robber. I stole this head, these arms and legs, this body from my master, and ran away with them." Then he asked the crowd, "Is this Negro before you a man or a thing?"

Elizabeth had planned on leaving right after Douglass finished speaking. But when he was done, Ann grabbed hold of her arm. She started to lead her over to the group of people talking with the abolitionist minister.

Elizabeth knew there was no turning back now. These people were doing what was right.

Elizabeth did not see Daryl until lunch the next day. As usual, he looked as if there were a lot of things on his mind. Elizabeth did not seem to be one of them.

"How was Washington?" she asked.

"Oh, well, a mess, really. The country is so close to war, and the president isn't doing anything."

"Any news of the election?"

"No. But Lincoln sounds stronger all the time."

"Do you think" she said, changing the subject, "we might have the evening together tonight?"

"I'm sorry. I'm not sure how long I'll have to be at the office." He didn't even look at her as he said this. Then he finished his lunch quickly and left the house.

Elizabeth was growing worried. Perhaps Daryl was getting tired of her. Maybe he was bored with their marriage. Or maybe . . . she could hardly finish the thought. Maybe he cared for someone else.

That afternoon Corinn showed a man into the drawing room. He wore a worn-out overcoat and had a thick beard. His head was covered with a large, funny-looking hat. Elizabeth threw a sharp look at Corinn. Why hadn't she told the man to wait at the door and then come and gotten her?

When Elizabeth asked the man how she could help him, he said, "I'd like to speak to you alone." Elizabeth nodded to Corinn. She didn't know who the man was. But she was not afraid of him.

As soon as Corinn left the room, the man took off his coat and hat. Elizabeth looked nervously at the door. She had not invited him to stay.

Then he began tearing off his beard! Standing before her was the abolitionist minister.

"I don't mean to alarm you," he said softly. "I'm so sorry to come this way. But I thought it was necessary. My name is David Sawyer."

"Yes, I know your name," Elizabeth said. "What do you want?"

"We need your help."

"Help? I'm sorry, but—"

David Sawyer held up a hand. "Hear me out. Please. I know from two people that you can be trusted."

"*Two*," thought Elizabeth. Certainly Ann was one. But who might the other be?

No one else knew her thoughts except, maybe . . .

"The slave hunters are on the trail of three runaways," the minister explained. "They are not safe where they are now. Even as we speak, they are in great danger. They have nowhere to go. The next station is no longer safe, either."

"I could get some food together, if that would help," Elizabeth said. "Or maybe even some clothing. I can do that, but that's all."

The minister took Elizabeth's hand and moved a step closer. "You must let these three people stay in your barn tonight. Because of your husband's position, no one will be suspicious."

"Oh, sir! That is impossible. I understand your commitment to this cause, Mr. Sawyer. I have even come to believe your cause is right and just. But you're asking me to risk not only my safety, but my husband's business."

"Ma'am, will you excuse me if I am bold?" the minister cut in. "I am talking about three *lives*. At this minute these people are being tracked by dogs and men with guns. You say you believe our cause is just. Then you *must* help us. I don't believe you will be in great danger. No one would think of looking for these runaways in your barn. It is only for one night. They will be gone tomorrow."

Elizabeth stood up from the chair. She walked across to the bookshelf and turned around. She looked the man squarely in the face. She knew he was right. If she really believed in the abolitionist movement, how could she not agree to help?

"All right," she said quietly. "I will do what I can."

"You're a brave woman, Mrs. Stellar."

"Oh, no, not so brave. I'm as frightened as I've ever been in my life." Elizabeth shook her head. "What do I have to do?"

David Sawyer spoke in a low voice. He told her every part of the plan. When he finished, he paused for a moment. Then he said, "There is something else, Mrs. Stellar. Corinn will be leaving with the group. You must act very surprised when the word gets out. If you must say anything, tell people you are angry. But don't overdo it. Be careful and talk as little as possible. And don't tell your husband a thing."

"But, how can I—" Elizabeth whispered.

"I must go now," the minister said, before she could finish. "Follow my instructions as closely as you possibly can."

Then he put his coat back on. He put the fake beard back on his face, and pulled the hat over his head. Elizabeth showed him to the door.

"At least Daryl will not be home tonight," Elizabeth thought. "Thank goodness for that."

She tried to keep away from Corinn for the rest of the day. She didn't know which was stronger: her admiration for, or her anger at Corinn. She was a brave woman. Elizabeth had to give her that. But why did she want to run away? They had been together their whole lives. Wasn't Corinn happy in their home? Even as Elizabeth asked these questions, she knew the answer. Corinn might be happy living in their home. But it wasn't a question of happiness. It was a question of freedom.

Finally, late in the afternoon, they bumped into each other in the hall.

"Ma'am?" Corinn said.

"I didn't say anything," Elizabeth said sharply.

Corinn started for the kitchen. Elizabeth called her back. It was stupid to pretend that nothing was going on.

"Corinn," she said. "We may as well get some food together. That is, if you haven't done it already. Make some corn bread and chicken. And get some apples, too."

"Ma'am?"

"Yes?"

"What about your husband?"

"Don't worry. Mr. Stellar won't be home until late tonight."

"Did I hear my name?"

Both women turned around to see Daryl entering the hall.

"You're home early!" Elizabeth nearly shouted.

Daryl looked a little puzzled, but then he smiled. "You sound disappointed," he said. "I thought I would surprise you. I brought my work home for the evening."

"Oh, no. I mean, that's wonderful. I'm so glad." How Elizabeth had longed for Daryl to surprise her like this. But not tonight! "I was just telling Corinn you wouldn't be home for supper," she said.

"But now you are. So she can make corn bread and chicken."

Elizabeth felt her face turning red. She wondered how much of the earlier conversation Daryl had heard. Had he heard only his name? Of all the nights for him to come home early!

The rest of the afternoon went by quickly. When they sat down to dinner, Elizabeth found that she could not eat. Twice her knife slipped from her hand and crashed on the plate.

"What's wrong, Elizabeth?" Daryl asked. "You seem so nervous."

"I'm not well, I guess."

"You should go to bed then. Here, let me help you upstairs."

"No!" she said too loudly and quickly. "I mean, I really want to stay up for a while. I'm not tired. My head hurts, that's all."

"As you please." Daryl's face looked tight and drawn.

"Tell me," Elizabeth began, trying to smooth out the tension between them. "Is anything new at the office?"

"Not so much really. Did you hear about Brian Murphy?"

"No."

"He caught five runaway slaves. That brought him a $3500 reward. And he picked up some extra money for turning in the folks that were hiding them."

"When?" she asked. She wondered if these were the slaves who were supposed to be coming to their barn tonight."

"Yesterday," Daryl said.

Elizabeth was relieved. It was a different group. Suddenly she remembered Martha Murphy looking around her backyard the other morning. Maybe Martha had known more about Corinn than Elizabeth had at the time. Maybe she should have mentioned Martha's nosing around to the minister.

Elizabeth just wanted the night to be over.

"I don't approve at all," Daryl went on to say. "What a way to make a living, slithering around like a snake. All this just so Martha can buy more furs."

"I think it's awful, too," Elizabeth answered. Her voice came out high and thin.

"They say there's a lot of money in it," Daryl went on. "More and more people are taking up slave chasing as if it were a sport." Daryl rubbed his head. Elizabeth noticed how tired he looked.

"I'll be up late tonight," Daryl said. He wiped his mouth with his napkin and started to leave the table.

Elizabeth knew it was time to start following the minister's instructions. She said "I'm going to send Corinn over to Ann's tonight. Ann is quite ill with a bad cold and fever. Corinn is so good at making special teas."

"That's a nice idea. I hope Ann gets well soon."

"Daryl, I was thinking that maybe you should write a note for Corinn. You know how things are now. It's not so safe for a slave to be out at night. But if she has a note from you saying where she is going, she will be all right."

"Oh, yes, of course," Daryl said. "That's a good idea. I'll do it right now."

Daryl left, and Elizabeth let out a long breath. Daryl bought the whole story. Elizabeth was surprised at how easy it was getting to lie to him.

Elizabeth saw Corinn to the door with her note and a large, full basket of food. "Be safe," Elizabeth whispered to her.

"Wait for the candle, no matter how late."

"Thank you, ma'am," Corinn said. Then the serious young woman smiled, something Elizabeth almost never saw her do. Elizabeth shut the door wondering how many people helped their own slaves run away.

The evening hours passed far too slowly. Elizabeth caught up on her sewing. Then she went to bed, so Daryl would not be suspicious.

"I'll be up for awhile," were his last words to her.

The hardest part was trying to stay awake as she lay in her bed. Sleep would be such sweet relief. In her mind, Elizabeth went over every step Corinn and the others were taking. She prayed they were safe.

From Ann's house, Corinn would go to the woods. There she would meet the three runaways. She would lead them through the woods to the edge of the Stellars' farm. They would wait in the darkness of the forest until they got the sign from Elizabeth that all was clear.

Finally, at midnight, Elizabeth heard Daryl go to bed. She waited another half hour for him to fall asleep. Then she crept out of bed. She tiptoed to his door and listened. He was breathing evenly, sleeping.

Only one more step to go.

Elizabeth took a candle from her bedroom. She carried it to a back room that had a window facing the woods. Elizabeth carefully placed the burning candle in the window and stepped back. She imagined Corinn and the others stepping out of the woods onto the field. Even without a moon, they could be seen in the starlight if anyone were watching. She imagined them moving quietly and quickly to the safety of the barn.

Elizabeth climbed back in her bed almost relieved. She had done her part. The runaways would have a good dinner and a safe night. By morning they would be gone.

She had begun to fall off to sleep when a shocking thought came to her. No one had told her how or when the group was going to leave the barn. And no one had told her where they were going to go.

Elizabeth awoke later that night. She opened her eyes. A figure was moving from the door to her bed. "Daryl?" she whispered.

"No, ma'am," came back another whisper. "It's me."

"Corinn? What is it? Is something wrong?"

"No. But please come out to the barn. We need your help."

"I can't do that! What if Daryl wakes up?"

"We'll have to be very quiet." The two women were speaking in whispers.

"Very well," Elizabeth said. As she brushed sleep from her eyes, she felt stronger. "Daryl sleeps soundly. But if he wakes up, I'll tell him I felt ill and called for you. I'll say you are going to make some tea and draw me a bath."

"Yes, ma'am," Corinn said.

The two women moved slowly and quietly through the upstairs hall. A loud groan came from Daryl's room. Then the sound of covers being thrown back.

"Elizabeth?" he called out.

"Yes, dear?" Elizabeth said.

"What are you doing up?"

She told him the story she and Corinn had agreed upon.

"Shall I call for a doctor?" Daryl asked.

"No, I'll be all right, dear. Go back to sleep."

As Elizabeth and Daryl talked, Corinn moved slowly down the hall. Elizabeth waited to make sure Daryl wasn't getting up. Within seconds, she heard the regular breathing of one who is asleep. She followed Corinn.

When they got downstairs, they went out the door and across the field to the barn. Elizabeth looked up at the stars. She picked the three brightest ones and made three wishes: for Daryl, for the runaways, and for herself.

Elizabeth and Corinn entered the barn. Inside they saw a small, tired looking woman standing with her feet planted apart and her head held up. Elizabeth could see the shiny barrel of a gun hanging down from the woman's hand. Elizabeth froze.

Corinn whispered to her. "Don't mind the gun, ma'am. Mrs. Tubman always carries one. It's just so she can protect herself."

"*Harriet* Tubman?" Elizabeth said too loudly.

"That's right," the small woman said. Her gaze was fixed on Elizabeth. Though the woman looked frail, her clear eyes showed she was in control. Harriet Tubman did not look like someone to cross. Elizabeth took a few steps back.

Sitting near the pile of hay were three more people—an elderly couple and Jonathan.

"Jonathan?" Elizabeth said, looking to Corinn. Everything was becoming clear now. Corinn smiled.

"These are my parents," Jonathan said to Elizabeth, waving to the old couple. "Mr. and Mrs. Bronson," he said, using their last name. This was not usually done in front of white people. Elizabeth saw that Jonathan was a proud man. That made her happy for Corinn, in spite of everything.

"Pleased to meet you," Elizabeth said. Jonathan stood and eyed her suspiciously. She could see that he did not trust her. And why should he? In a second, she could lose for him his parents, the woman he loved, and his own freedom. Elizabeth silently promised to do whatever was asked of her.

"No time for nice talk," Mrs. Tubman said. "You probably know that the slave catchers have had some success around here," she said to Elizabeth. "I'm proud to say that I've made more than a dozen trips on the underground railroad. And I've never lost a passenger. We must leave tomorrow. Those white men are probably moving from barn to farmhouse to barn looking for us. There is no time to lay over, even though these old people need some rest." She pointed at Jonathan's parents. "I think we should move by the light of day tomorrow. People are less suspicious during the day."

"That's where you come in," Mrs. Tubman added, looking right at Elizabeth.

"What do I have to do?" Elizabeth asked.

"I want you to drive us to the next station tomorrow morning," Mrs. Tubman said. "It's twenty miles down the road in the town of Wilder, just across the McCall River. We will ride in the wagon under a load of hay."

"But people know me!" Elizabeth said. "It would look very strange for me to be driving a wagon."

"Can you handle a wagon and horse?" Mrs. Tubman asked.

"Well, yes," Elizabeth said. She thought back to her childhood on the farm. She had ridden better than her brothers much of the time. But that was years ago.

"You can dress as a boy so no one will know you," Mrs. Tubman said. "I've done it myself many times. I'd do it this time, but we need a white face."

Elizabeth looked at the runaways one by one. Mrs. Tubman, Corinn, Jonathan, and his parents. Slowly she nodded her head. She was ready for this job. Already she could feel the reins in her hands. And she could hear the heavy clop-clop of the horses feet. They were keeping time with the beating of her heart.

6

The next morning Daryl left for work at his usual time, seven o'clock. As soon as he had gone, Elizabeth went to his room. She found an old pair of his pants and tried them on. They were far too big.

She took out her sewing box and set to work. She only had about an hour-and-a-half to get ready. Harriet Tubman had said they would begin at 8:30.

When Elizabeth was finished, she pulled on the pants. They fit well enough. She found an old shirt that could pass for a boy's.

Then, she practiced being a boy for a little while. First she walked around the room. She tried to let her arms and legs move loosely. Next she tried her voice. The first time she spoke, it sounded too low for a boy. She tried again and felt that was better. She figured she could pass for a 14-year-old boy.

The last touch was to tie up her hair and put on a big straw hat. "Oh, no!" she cried into the mirror. Anyone could see that her long hair was pulled up under the hat.

There was only one thing she could do. And she only had a few moments to do it.

Elizabeth quickly found her sewing scissors. She took hold of the locks of hair that grew at the top of her neck. These were the ones that showed below the hat. She cut them a length of one inch.

"There," she said, admiring her work. With the back of her hair cut short, no one would dream she was a woman. Then, later on, the rest of her hair would fall over the cut part. No one would ever know.

Elizabeth smiled. She was almost enjoying herself. If only she had David Sawyer's fake beard!

Now dressed completely in men's clothes, Elizabeth slipped downstairs. She would go out the back door where no one would see her. But just as she was shutting the door behind her, she heard something. It was the sound of voices in Corinn's cottage.

Elizabeth knew it couldn't be the Bronsons. They would have stayed in the barn. She was sure of that. Elizabeth moved slowly and silently toward the cottage. She hid behind some brush nearby and listened. She could hear the conversation clearly now.

One of the voices was Corinn's. And she sounded upset. The other voice was deep, but also a woman's. Elizabeth was afraid to admit to herself that that voice sounded familiar.

"I know you know where they are," the deep-voiced woman said. "I've seen you talking to Jonathan in town. I know there's something between you."

"I don't know what you're talking about," Corinn said.

"Yes you do," the woman said." And I think you will tell me. If you don't, some unpleasant things could happen to you. *Very* unpleasant."

"I would help you if I could," Corinn answered calmly. "I have no idea where Jonathan is."

"I think you'll regret this, Corinn. And if you tell anyone about our conversation, you'll regret it even more."

Elizabeth crept quietly back to the house. She took off the boy's clothing and put on one of her own dresses. She brushed her long hair over the short back parts. Then she rushed back downstairs and out the back door.

"Corinn? Corinn?" she called. "Where are you?"

Corinn came out of the cottage followed by Martha Murphy.

"I'm sorry you had to find out this way," Martha said. "I thought Corinn and I could settle it ourselves. But since you are here, I must talk to you. I suppose it was my duty in the first place. Mr. Murphy caught Corinn stealing from the store in town. Didn't he, Corinn?"

"Yes, ma'am," Corinn lied.

"I came here to speak to her about it directly," said Martha, her nose sniffing the air.

Elizabeth swallowed a gasp. Sneaking around and lying like a thief. What had become of Martha? She used to be her friend.

Elizabeth followed Corinn's lead. They must both play the game very well now.

"Corinn," Elizabeth said as sternly as she could. "Wait in your cottage until I come speak to you." Corinn went back into the cottage with her head down.

Martha trailed Elizabeth into the house. "I'm so sorry to bring you this news. It's just awful, I know."

"You were only doing your duty, Martha," Elizabeth said.

Martha gave her old friend a questioning look. Then she put on a smile. "I must be going. By the way, did you hear that Jonathan from the Goodall's farm has run away?"

"No!" Elizabeth cried. Her hand flew to her throat.

"They've put up a $1500 reward for the return of him and his parents."

"Is that so?" Elizabeth said coolly. She noticed that Martha had on a new dress. She and Brian seemed to have come into a lot of money lately.

"As you know," Martha continued, "Brian has taken it on as his neighborly duty to look for runaways. He and his committee will have Jonathan by this afternoon. I'm sure of it. They cannot have gotten far yet. Why, I bet they are hiding within five miles of us right now." Martha smiled. "I must be off. Good day!"

Elizabeth raced upstairs to change back into the boy's clothes. She was late now. She wondered how much Martha knew. Perhaps she knew about the whole plan. Perhaps she was just playing cat and mouse with Elizabeth and Corinn. They must move—and move fast.

Elizabeth took one last look at herself in the mirror. She was ready, except for one thing. She pulled a box out from under her bed. In the box she found a small gold bracelet. Her mother had given it to her when Elizabeth was twelve. As a child she had always believed it was magic, that it brought her good luck. Elizabeth slipped the bracelet in a pocket. She hurried toward the barn.

"Ready to go, Jumper?" Elizabeth said to the horse as she entered the barn. This sentence was the signal to the runaways that everything was clear.

First Jonathan crawled out from under the hay. Then came Harriet Tubman. They both helped Jonathan's parents out.

"Where's Corinn?" Jonathan asked nervously. "She was supposed to be here a while ago."

"She'll be here," Elizabeth answered. She didn't want to tell anyone what had happened with Martha. It would only make them more worried. Elizabeth hoped that Corinn was only waiting a little longer to make certain Martha didn't return.

"We won't leave without her," Jonathan said.

"We have to leave right away," Mrs. Tubman ordered.

"I won't go without Corinn." Jonathan started for the door.

"Get back here," cried Elizabeth. If one person spotted Jonathan, they were all dead. And there were spies everywhere.

Harriet Tubman lunged after Jonathan. The small woman looked as if she planned to wrestle the six-foot Jonathan to the ground.

Just in time, Corinn ran into the barn. Jonathan quickly hugged her. Mrs. Tubman grabbed and pushed the two of them toward the wagon.

Elizabeth took the pitchfork and threw some hay in the wagon bed. Jonathan helped his parents get in. Then he and Corinn climbed in. Mrs. Tubman and Elizabeth covered them with a huge pile of hay.

Elizabeth climbed into the driver's seat. "What about you?" she said to Mrs. Tubman.

"I'm not going," Mrs. Tubman said. "I have some more work to do before heading back north. Thanks for the offer, anyway."

"You can't stay here," Elizabeth said.

"I won't be here much longer," Mrs. Tubman answered. "Now you must leave." Elizabeth nodded and shook the reins. They were on their way.

Once they were on the road, Elizabeth pressed Jumper to go faster. She enjoyed the feeling of sitting high on the wagon, with the reins in her hands. She felt big and strong, like she had felt as a child racing her brothers.

Five miles out of town, Elizabeth heard the gallop of horses coming up behind her. She turned and saw two men riding to catch up with her. Suddenly she was frightened. Brian Murphy would surely recognize her, even in boy's clothes.

Elizabeth reached down to the floorboard. The wooden wagon was muddy. She wiped some dirt across her face. Anything to cover up as much as she could. The sound of galloping horses filled her ears.

"Morning, son!" The men on horses were beside her now. Elizabeth slowly turned to look at them. With relief, she didn't recognize either man.

"Morning," she said in a low voice.

"That hay must be as heavy as rocks at the speed you're going," the man said. He laughed and looked at his friend.

"Horses are lazy these days," the man said back. "Can't get them to work."

Elizabeth couldn't tell if they were suspicious of anything. Maybe they were just joking around.

The first man said, "We're looking for a runaway named Jonathan. He's about six feet tall. He's probably with two old people."

"Good luck to you," Elizabeth said. "I hope you find him. I haven't seen anyone like that on the road this morning."

"Brian Murphy said he might be running away with the Stellars' girl, Corinn. We were just at the Stellars' house. But all we found was an old black woman asleep in their barn."

Elizabeth felt her face get hot. "An old woman? What was she doing there?"

"I don't know," one of the men said.

"The Stellars must have hired a little extra help. She looked so weak, though, she can't be much good to anyone. She jumped up and began pitching hay like crazy when we came in." The man threw back his head and laughed when he said this. "Scared of getting caught sleeping on the job, I guess."

"Guess so," Elizabeth said. "Just an old woman," Elizabeth thought. "To weak to be much good to anyone!" This was not the first time Harriet Tubman had had the last laugh. Elizabeth didn't think it would be the last time, either.

"Thanks anyway," the men said. "Have a good ride."

Elizabeth was so pleased with her acting, she began to tip her hat. Then she thought better of it. She could just see her long hair spilling down.

The men swung their horses around and rode back toward town. This was not a good sign. Surely the two men would report this conversation to someone. Elizabeth had no idea how much Martha Murphy knew. But she bet the "committee" was not finished checking out her house. The faster she went and the farther away she got, the safer they would all be.

After about ten miles, the road entered the forest. Dark clouds began to fill the sky. Soon there was no blue showing at all. Elizabeth shivered. She had no jacket.

A few drops of rain began to fall. In minutes, it was raining hard. Elizabeth worried about Jonathan's parents. Because of their age, the rain and cold would bother them more. The horse slowed down, unwilling to go fast in the rain.

No one else was on the road. Elizabeth kept looking over her shoulder, expecting at any moment to see that she was being followed. She was relieved each time she saw the empty stretch of road behind her. Even so, she felt lonely. And she was shaking with cold.

Suddenly, a rider on a horse galloped out of the woods behind them. The rider was leaning forward and riding fast, trying to catch the wagon.

This was it. Elizabeth stood up and shook the reins. Jumper began to run. "Get up! Get up!" she cried to the horse.

But it was no use. The rider wasn't pulling a heavy wagon. In a few moments he was riding next to her.

"Look at me," the man shouted at her. The rain was beating down on her straw hat so loudly Elizabeth could hardly hear. She knew it was hopeless trying to get away from him, so she slowed down. Then she turned to face him.

The man had a full black beard. His hair was also black under his hat. But his eyes were sky blue. It was the minister, David Sawyer!

"Listen carefully," he said speaking as loudly as he could. "Murphy and his boys are on your trail. You spoke with two men who mentioned you to Murphy. He's riding out to check up on you. He and his friends will question you and probably search the wagon."

"They'll recognize me!"

"Yes," said Sawyer. "You must leave the wagon and horse. You'll have to go the last five miles on foot and through the woods. Stay off the road until you get to Wilder. Also, stay away from the bridge across the McCall River. It's watched 24 hours a day. Go at least a mile upriver and swim across."

"But I can't—"

"There's no time for talk now. Murphy and his boys are close behind. Do as I say. Here's a gun. If at any time someone stops you, say you are a slave catcher. Make up different names for the Bronsons and Corinn and say you are taking them to their owner in Wilder. I know you can do it. Be careful and God be with you. Go now."

Elizabeth jumped down from the driver's seat. Sawyer tied his horse in with Jumper. As he got in the driver's seat, the Bronsons and Corinn climbed out of the hay.

"Come on," Elizabeth said. "The longer we stay out here in the road, the greater the chances are that we'll be caught." The group of five hurried through the pounding rain into the darkness of the forest.

CHAPTER

7

Everyone was wet and cold. It was nearly impossible to walk quickly through the woods. There were big logs to step over. As the five of them walked, their feet sank in the piles of soggy leaves. A wind blew the cold rain into their faces.

The group tried to keep the road in sight so they would not get lost. At the same time, they didn't want to be seen. It was important to blend in with the forest as much as squirrels did. The going was slow.

Mrs. Bronson began to have trouble keeping up. Corinn and Elizabeth each held one of the older woman's arms. Elizabeth thought her arm would break where the big woman hung onto it.

"What's that sound?" Jonathan said, and stopped walking. He reached for

Corinn and pulled her to him. Elizabeth heard horses on the road. Then she could hear men's voices, too.

"I hear something," one of the men on the road said. "Over there in the woods."

Jonathan began sinking to his knees very slowly. He nodded for everyone to do the same. Without making a sound, they lowered themselves to the ground where they would be out of sight. The pounding of Elizabeth's heart sounded louder than a drumroll in her ears.

"Which way?" another man on the road asked. "We'll set the dogs loose."

"Forget it," said a voice that Elizabeth recognized. It was Brian Murphy. "They could never have gotten this far on foot. And the only wagon that has gone out on the road this morning was the one we checked. Let's head back to town. I bet they left by the southern road."

The sounds from the road faded into the distance. Murphy and his friends had turned back.

Jonathan bent over and lifted his mother. Elizabeth saw his face draw up in pain. He lifted the big woman on his back, placing her arms around his neck.

The group set out once more. Soon it

became obvious that Mr. Bronson was also going to need help. Elizabeth and Corinn each put one of his arms around their own necks. He was much lighter than his wife. The two women were able to move him along, even if his feet had to drag a little.

As she moved slowly, sweating and gasping for air, Elizabeth felt she had been here before. The barking of dogs. The shouting of men's voices. The darkness of the forest.

Then she remembered her dream. This was it. The dream had told her of the work she would be called on to do. And deep inside herself she had known it all along.

Finally, the group reached the banks of the McCall River. They were just one mile above the bridge. Once they got across the river, they would be only one mile from the town of Wilder. There they would find safety.

The group stood for a minute and looked across to the other side of the muddy water.

Suddenly, Corinn burst into tears. "Oh, Jonathan," she cried. "Not one of us can swim."

The river was moving quickly. Elizabeth knew the water was icy. A person could be swept away in a second.

"We will now," Jonathan said, his eyes fixed on the far bank. "Today we will learn to swim."

"Yes," said Elizabeth. She put an arm around Corinn. "Perhaps it's not too deep."

Elizabeth waited with Jonathan's parents as Jonathan and Corinn went first. They waded out slowly. Their clothes had already been soaked by the rain.

With each step, the water moved higher up on their bodies. Elizabeth knew the tug of the water was strong. Slowly, step-by-step, they went deeper. The water moved up around Jonathan's middle. He had a tight grip on Corinn's arm.

How much deeper would it get?

With the next few steps the water went back down to Jonathan's hips! They had been through the deepest part. Soon it was at his knees. Now they were on the far bank.

Elizabeth cried. Tears of joy washed down her face along with the rainwater. The river was not over their heads. They did not have to swim. Jonathan plunged into the river again, and waded back across quickly.

Elizabeth helped Mr. Bronson across as Jonathan helped his mother. Jonathan went back a last time for the gun. On the far bank they all hugged one another. Now, they had only to get through the streets of Wilder to the general store.

"Look mean," Jonathan said to Elizabeth with a grin. He handed her the gun. At first she looked at it in her hands as if it were a dead animal. Then she held it as she thought a man would. And they set off to walk into town.

When they reached Wilder, Elizabeth was surprised that they caught no one's eye. Then she realized that their wet clothes didn't give them away. It was still raining hard. Everyone in the streets was wet. On the far side of Main Street, Elizabeth spotted the general store.

"Ma'am!" Jonathan said to her. Elizabeth realized she had begun to break into a run. Never in her life had she wanted anything more than to be behind the doors of that store.

The others waited outside while Elizabeth went in. Behind the counter stood a tall, thin man. He wore small glasses and had white hair. There were several customers in the store.

"May I help you?" asked the man.

"Yes." Elizabeth used her best boy's voice. "I have a delivery to make. Uh, the hay you asked for."

Saying this was part of her instructions. She realized now, though, that there was no wagon of hay outside. She hoped none of the customers would notice.

"Go around to the back," the man said. He smiled warmly, and pointed out the door.

Elizabeth stepped back out in the rain. The Bronsons and Corinn were gone! She looked up and down the street. They had disappeared into thin air.

Something tugged at her shirt. Elizabeth looked down at a small boy, about eight years old. He said nothing to her. But he pulled at her shirt again. She followed him to the back of the store.

There he took her into what looked like a woodshed. Behind a small pile of wood, though, was another door. This led to a secret room in back of the store.

The silent boy pushed her in and slipped in after her.

Before Elizabeth was the most welcome sight in her life. The runaways were already seated at a big table. A small fire was crackling in a fireplace. Elizabeth saw that the fireplace shared a chimney with the one in the store.

"You must be Mrs. Stellar," said a woman with a kind face. "I am Mrs. Oakley. Thank goodness you are all safe. Sit down."

Mrs. Oakley had a hot meal ready for them in no time. Elizabeth and the others fell on the food like vultures. Without a word they ate and drank. When a plate was empty, Mrs. Oakley filled it. Knowing how tired and hungry they were, she asked no questions.

Soon Mr. Oakley, the man in the store, slipped into the room. "Welcome to the Wilder station of the underground railroad," he said. "You are safe here. We have cots for you to sleep on. Later, we will talk about the next leg of your journey."

Elizabeth saw Corinn nod silently. She and Jonathan had not let go of each other's hands since they arrived at the Oakley's.

"I understand that you must get home before your husband tonight, Mrs. Stellar," Mr. Oakley said. "My grandson has gotten a fresh horse ready for you. Someone will come to get it from your barn tonight."

"You had better hurry," Mrs. Oakley said. "I wish I had dry clothes I could give you. But here, take this jacket." Elizabeth put on the men's jacket. It was too big, but it was warm.

"I would like to talk to Corinn alone for a minute," Elizabeth said before she left. She looked around the room. It was too small for a private conversation. So she went ahead and said, "I just wanted to wish you and Jonathan much happiness."

Corinn nodded and answered, "Thank you, ma'am. We will never forget what you have done for us."

Elizabeth reached in her pocket. She pulled out the gold bracelet. "I'd like you to have this. For good luck. Good-bye."

When Elizabeth went outside, she was pleased to see that the rain had stopped. She was able to ride hard all the way back to her farm. She arrived home just minutes before Daryl was expected. She put her horse in the barn. Then she ran across the wet field toward the warm house and dry clothes.

Home! As Elizabeth went in the back door she wanted to cry out in joy. By the time Daryl got home she would be all cleaned up and have on a dress. She began to climb the stairs to her bedroom. At the top of the stairs she suddenly realized how tired she was.

"What are you doing!" a man shouted.

Elizabeth whirled around. Daryl was standing at the bottom of the long flight of stairs.

"Don't move," he said. His face was filled with anger. He moved slowly up the stairs toward her. "I'm going to check your pockets and then take you to the police."

Elizabeth realized Daryl didn't recognize her. Only her cut hair showed under the big straw hat. She still had mud all over her face. And she was wearing the heavy men's jacket Mrs. Oakley had given her.

Elizabeth had to think fast now. If Daryl got any closer, he would recognize her. Elizabeth knew Daryl didn't keep a gun in the house. She would have a chance if she ran. She turned and took off toward the back bedroom. She opened the door to the servant's stairs. Down she flew. Daryl was close on her heels shouting, "Thief! Thief!"

At the bottom of the servant's stairs Elizabeth slammed the door shut. She raced out the back door and slammed that behind her, too. She knew the back garden much better than Daryl. She went to a far corner where she had not yet done any work. The brush was thick. Elizabeth climbed in behind it.

She got there just in time. Daryl came running out the back door. Elizabeth lay as still as she could. She held her breath. Instead of searching the garden, Daryl ran out in the road.

Minutes later, he was back. He was talking to himself, angrily. She knew he would search the house for anything missing. Then he would go to the police. That's when she could get back in the house.

Elizabeth was terribly cold. She lay in the brush wondering about her life. Chased like a thief by her own husband! Would life ever be normal for them again? Would she ever be able to tell him what she had done?

It seemed that hours had passed when Elizabeth heard Daryl finally leave the house. It had probably only been a few minutes. She crawled out of the brush and crept inside.

Elizabeth threw off the boy's clothes and hid them. Then she washed up and got in bed. Daryl had not discovered her. Yet.

The next morning Elizabeth did not get out of bed. She had a bad cold and a high fever.

"I've been worried you would get sick," Daryl said to her. "It's my fault. I've been away from home so much." He said nothing about the thief. Nor did he ask where she had been in the early evening when he had come home yesterday.

"I've missed you," Elizabeth said. Her head was completely stuffed up and she was still very tired.

"Where is Corinn?" Daryl asked. "I'll have her make you some tea," Daryl said.

"I'm not sure exactly where she is," Elizabeth answered.

"I'll get her."

As Daryl started downstairs, Elizabeth heard someone knocking on the door. When Daryl answered it, she heard Priscilla's voice.

"Oh! I heard the news!" Priscilla sang out in her high voice.

"What news?" asked Daryl.

"What news! About Corinn, of course. What are you going to do? Is Elizabeth *very* upset? I just can't imagine how Corinn slipped out under your very eyes. I mean, really—"

"Hold on, hold on," Daryl said. "What in the world are you talking about?"

As Elizabeth lay in bed she could just picture Priscilla's eyes getting wide.

"You don't know?" Priscilla squealed. "Why, Martha Murphy said she knows for a fact that Corinn ran away with Jonathan from the Goodall's farm. Go look for yourself. Corinn is not out in the cottage."

"Well, good morning!" This time Elizabeth recognized Martha's voice. "It is my duty to tell you, Daryl, that Corinn has run away. When Brian couldn't find Jonathan yesterday, I came looking for you and Elizabeth. I couldn't find either of you. So I searched Corinn's cottage, and she was gone! She must have run away with Jonathan while you two were out yesterday. I am sorry to be the one to bring you this news."

That was the last thing Elizabeth heard before she passed out. The next thing she knew, she was bathed in sweat and Daryl was wiping her face with a cold cloth.

Later, when Elizabeth felt a little better, Daryl told her what Priscilla and Martha had had to say. He sighed deeply as he sat on the edge of her bed.

"Martha wanted to know how much money we will give for her return," Daryl said.

"Oh, we won't do that, will we?" Elizabeth asked.

"No," Daryl said quietly. "The Goodalls are making enough of a scene about Jonathan and his parents. The important thing for us now is that you get well."

Elizabeth stayed in bed for a week. She would not see any visitors. Most people in town thought she was upset about Corinn's running away. When she showed herself in town again, people whispered quietly as she passed. But no one questioned her about Corinn.

While Elizabeth was sick in bed, Daryl had been very sweet and attentive. It was almost like old times. Elizabeth had decided she could no longer live with her lie. She had to tell Daryl everything. War between the North and South was almost certain now. The time had come to take sides, and she knew where she stood.

Two weeks after Elizabeth's journey to Wilder, there was another abolitionist meeting. She wanted to go. She would talk to Daryl first, though. She would tell him everything.

That night they sat down to dinner. Daryl was acting strangely again, as if his thoughts were far away.

"Daryl," Elizabeth began. "I must tell you something very important."

"Yes, dear?" Daryl did not look at her. He was eating his chicken quickly.

"It is about Corinn."

"I know. You need some help. Of course you can't do all the work."

"No, it's not that. I'm happy doing the work."

"Can we talk later?" Daryl got up and pushed in his chair. "I have a meeting."

"Daryl!" Elizabeth jumped up to face him. "Can't we ever talk?" Her eyes filled with tears.

"I'm sorry," he said. "First thing in the morning, all right?"

"Fine," Elizabeth said, her voice cracking. "In the morning."

Daryl left and Elizabeth did the dishes quickly. She had a meeting tonight herself. If her marriage was going to fall apart, at least she would have her work. She knew Ann would always be there for her, too.

Elizabeth entered the store where the secret meeting was being held. So far she had only gone to the two public meetings. Now she was being asked to the secret ones where the real planning was done. The room was packed. There were both black and white people there.

Since the meeting hadn't started, people were talking in small groups. Elizabeth found Ann near the door and fell into her arms. "Oh, Elizabeth," Ann cried. "I heard what you did, though I wasn't supposed to know. I'm so proud of you. You are the bravest woman I know."

"Was it you who put them up to asking me?" Elizabeth asked. She was still a little angry about that part.

"No. You should know I wouldn't do that. The only thing I did was answer 'yes' when David Sawyer asked if you were to be trusted. I didn't know for what. Until later."

"Then it was Corinn?"

Ann nodded. "She knew where your heart lay."

"My heart also lies with my husband," Elizabeth said. Then she couldn't stop the tears. They overflowed. A few people near them turned and stared.

"But Elizabeth!" Ann took her friend by the shoulders. "Surely you know!"

"Know what?" Elizabeth asked, her voice husky from crying. She looked up at Ann and was surprised to see her friend laughing.

"Oh, my, we are *too* good at keeping secrets! Come with me, Elizabeth." Ann led Elizabeth through the crowd. "I have someone I want you to meet."

The next time Elizabeth looked up she was looking into the surprised face of her own husband. "Daryl?" she whispered. "What are you doing here?"

"What are *you* doing here?" he shot back.

"I thought you two had come together!" Ann said.

Elizabeth and Daryl stared at each other in disbelief. Then Daryl took her hand and led her through the people to the door. Outside on the street they stared at each other silently for several moments.

Finally, a smile appeared at the corner of Elizabeth's mouth. "Is this why . . . ?" she began.

"I'm beginning to understand quite a bit, I think," Daryl said.

Elizabeth laughed. "Oh, I think there is probably quite a bit you don't understand!" She thought of the runaways in the barn, her journey, Daryl chasing her.

"We have a lot to talk about," Daryl said.

"I tried to talk this evening."

Daryl lowered his head. "I'm sorry. I have been so afraid to tell you what was on my mind. This abolitionist work means the end of my job, you know. It may mean selling our home, a complete change in our lives. I was so afraid you would never understand. I hardly understand it myself! How will we live?"

Elizabeth smiled once more. Her future had never been more uncertain. Yet her heart had never been lighter. She took Daryl's hand and pulled him toward home. They could miss this meeting tonight. There would be many more. For now, they had a lot of catching up to do.

A Test of Loyalty

S. D. Jones

CHAPTER

1

'

The train ride to Oregon was a peaceful one. Too peaceful for restless, young Harry Drewes. His mother, Olive Dunford Drewes, had seen to it that he got the best compartment. She always made sure he was well fed and looked after.

The owner of the train line was a friend of Olive's. She had written him to make sure his people would treat Harry well.

Harry watched the plains of Nebraska go by. He felt sorry for himself. This was not the trip he had hoped for. He had wanted adventure—not the porters and the room service. Back in New York, he had pictured himself riding in a freight car. How else would he be able to write about life?

Instead, the velvet on the seat and the clacking of the rail kept putting him to sleep.

Though he felt guilty, he allowed himself the rest. But he was determined to stay awake through the Rockies. This was the West! It might not be the wild and wide-open West of a half century ago. After all, this was 1920. But to Harry it was all new and very exciting.

How often had he heard of Hattie Pryce's life, growing up in the West more then 70 years ago. Harry had never known this woman, who had died long ago. But Hattie's daughter, Harry's Great-Aunt Mary, had passed along Hattie's journal.

Harry was so inspired, he started keeping his own journal. He was writing in it now. That was the purpose of this trip after all—to write about life. That was *his* purpose anyway.

As the train rolled on Harry wrote:

"All I have ever known is New York. A wilderness full of people. An island with too many bridges. I've known only cars, trolleys, noise and hustle-bustle. Riding on this train I am free. I am beginning my adventure . . ."

His mother had *other* ideas, of course. But she was not on the train. So Harry was free to do as he wished.

Many images of Oregon filled his head. He could almost see the rolling hills, bright sunshine, and open spaces. He wondered what the paper mill would look like. Would the workers there like him? Would he like them?

Would they be a rough and tumble sort of people? Would they have stories to tell? He hoped so. To 19-year-old Harry Drewes, life was a great story about to unfold. And he would be its hero.

The train rode on, with the sound of clicketyclacks and whistles filling Harry's head. It wouldn't be long now.

The train reached Redfield two days later at 4:00 P.M. Carl Franklin was already waiting for Harry when he stepped down from the train.

Harry recognized Franklin from his mother's description. "Tall, thin, like a beanpole," his mother had said. "And he has dark hair and a big, dark mustache that covers his upper lip."

At first glance, Harry thought he was a rather hard chap. But as they walked out of the train station, Carl smiled. He took Harry's luggage and warmly patted him on the back.

"Welcome Harry," said Carl. "Come with me. You must be hungry."

Harry didn't have a chance to answer, for Carl was already leading him toward a horse and buggy.

"Sorry," said Carl. "There are not many automobiles here in Redfield, Oregon. We still get around the old-fashioned way." He laughed and motioned for the driver to get going.

Harry couldn't help staring at the driver. He was an odd man, distant and cold—and big. But his eyes were small and filled with suspicion. He had an ugly scar on his right cheek. Carl noticed that Harry was staring.

"Oh, don't mind Josh here," Carl said to Harry. "He's my right-hand man. Don't talk much, but he's strong as an ox. Right, Josh?"

Carl slapped the driver hard on the back, but the big man didn't turn around. He seemed to take no notice of Harry or Carl.

Carl Franklin lived just a few blocks from the train station in a large and important-looking house. A porch wrapped around the front and there were large double doors to the entrance. Harry liked the house right away. He had lived in an apartment in the city his whole life.

Harry changed clothes and washed up as soon as he arrived. When he came downstairs, he saw that the dinner table was set and a maid was bringing out food.

"Come on, Harry," Carl said. "Your mother wrote and told me you eat like a horse. Is that true?" he winked and smiled.

"Well, I—"

"I hope so. I have the cupboards all stocked. Don't disappoint me."

Carl motioned for Harry to sit, as he began to cut a large roast.

"So tell me," said Carl, "how's your family? How's Olive?"

"My mother's fine, thank you," said Harry.

"She tells me you want to learn some management skills."

"Actually, I—"

"Couldn't have come to a better place," said Carl. "The mill here employs 350 men full time, and many of their family members as well. I do a pretty good job of keeping them in line. But if your mother thinks I could use a little help—"

"No, no. It's not that," Harry said quickly. "Mother thinks the mill is doing fine. Really. It's just that ever since Grandpa Jefferson was killed—"

For the first time Carl frowned. He looked angry. "Jefferson was a good man," he said. "It pains me to think that some drunken unionists killed him. Bomb blast, wasn't it?"

"Yes," Harry answered. "But they never really proved who—"

"It was the workers. Bet on it. Not all of them are shifty and lazy, but the ones who are, you've got to watch like a hawk. Let your Grandpa's murder be a lesson to you, son."

Harry was only 19, but he never liked being called "son." "Actually, one of the reasons I came was to get to know the workers," Harry said. "I want to see how other people live, to get my hands dirty."

"Well," said Carl, "I see you are your father's boy as much as your mother's. It's the artist in you. Talk to the men as much as you like. But if you're here to help *me*, then my advice is not to get involved with them. Getting too chummy with your employees is no good. It'll only cause trouble. The workers here respect only fear. You try to act like one of them, and they'll eat you alive."

There was little use in talking, Harry felt. Carl's feelings about workers seemed to be set. Carl continued to talk on and on about the workers and unions and radicals. Harry sat in silence.

At bedtime, Harry walked upstairs to his room. Tomorrow would be a busy day at the mill. Harry wanted to be ready for it.

His bed was soft and comfortable. Very comfortable, indeed, thought Harry. He had been comfortable all his life. His whole life had been soft. Something inside him longed to break free. He was determined to get past all the velvet and silk.

Before falling asleep, Harry wrote one last entry in his journal:

"Arrived in Redfield. Mr. Franklin seems nice. Haven't seen the business or the workers yet. How odd it seems to be in the middle of this wild country and yet live in such luxury! Tomorrow, I meet the people who labor at the mill. I am nervous, but excited."

CHAPTER

2

Harry's education in life began the next day. He found the paper mill to be a hard place. As the days and weeks went by, Harry learned more and more about the mill. He learned how it worked, and how Carl managed the people. Harry found him to be a tough man who treated his workers harshly. Still, with help from Josh, Carl kept the mill running like a clock. Harry found time to speak with only a few workers. Carl never let him get too close to them.

One morning, after breakfast, Carl showed Harry the company's books.

"I do most of the work myself," Carl said proudly.

Harry didn't take much interest in numbers, but he could guess why Carl

was showing him the books. He wanted
to let Harry know that he was running
the business well. Carl knew that Harry
often wrote home. He wanted Harry to give
a good report.

After leaving Carl, Harry walked outside
and looked around. He never liked the
look of the mill. Of course he had seen
his grandfather's factories, warehouses,
and mills before. He had often toured them
with his mother. But they were in the
city. Buildings such as these seemed to
belong to the city landscape.

The mill here was different. It too was
made of dark red bricks and had gray
streets. In the city, these colors all went
together. But in the country, the mill
looked out of place. It looked huge and
angry against the rolling green hills, Harry
thought.

And the smell! The smell of the paper
mill was awful. Harry never could get used
to it.

"This mill is a regular powerhouse," Carl
said. "First trees are cut down and
stripped. It's the wood pulp method. A bit
old-fashioned, I know, but it's all
mechanical. The wood is bleached,
washed, and refined—all here."

By now the mill was a familiar sight to Harry. But he remembered the first time he had seen it. From the outside, the place had looked empty. No one walked around the grounds—they weren't allowed. At the mill, you either worked, ate, or went home.

Once inside, Harry couldn't believe his ears. The noise was hard to take. He thought back to the factories in the city. He remembered they had been noisy too. But this was different. Just outside the birds were chirping. The wind was rustling through the trees. Inside, Harry had to put his hands over his ears. A person could go deaf.

Now, weeks later, Harry knew his way around the mill pretty well. He walked by the area where they cut the wood. Saws whined and snarled here. Harry kept on walking. The next area was noisy, but nothing like the last place. Carl walked up and handed him a mask.

"Here, put this around your mouth," he said, then pointed to his chest. "Saves your lungs," he explained. Harry saw the logic in that. Here, they steamed the wood before crushing and beating it. Sawdust filled the air and foul smelling steam hung everywhere.

Harry looked at the workers and they stared back, scowling through suspicious eyes. He wondered what they were thinking. Then he realized that the workers were not wearing masks.

Later Harry was watching the cooking process when Carl called to him. He wanted to see him in the office. But Harry couldn't move. He felt something stick in his throat and he started to cough. He bent forward and threw off his mask. He gagged. Josh saw him and called for Carl.

Carl and Josh took hold of Harry and helped him to an outside courtyard.

"Are you all right, Harry?" asked Carl.

Harry continued to cough and gag. Finally he was able to say that he would be fine.

Carl sat Harry down on a step. Some workers were standing outside smoking and talking on a break. When Harry looked up he saw that they were staring at him.

Carl noticed as well, and he shouted "You people have nothing better to do than gawk? Get yourselves back to work."

The workers turned away just as a man came running through the crowd. "Mr. Franklin!" he yelled. "Mr. Franklin! We've got a grindstone problem on machine six. We're going to need some help."

Carl looked upset. He looked down at Harry and said, "You feel up to taking a look with me?"

Harry wanted to go along. He didn't want to seem like a baby. But he couldn't go on. The violent coughing had left him weak.

"I think I'll just sit here for a minute," Harry said.

"All right, you take it easy," Carl said. "Just sit here till we get back. Come on, Josh. I want you in there with me." Carl pushed Josh on ahead of him.

Harry watched as the two men went around the corner, out of sight. Once more the workers all turned toward him. Harry felt embarrassed. It was like being the new kid in class. They all looked at him but no one said a word. A few minutes passed like hours. Harry wanted to introduce himself, and if he had found one friendly face he would have.

Then a woman walked out of the group of workers. Harry figured that she was only a few years older than he was. She was fairly short, just over five feet. Her eyes were green and full of life. She wore a simple navy blue dress and a handkerchief covered her head. The most striking thing about her was her bright red hair.

"You the owner's kid?" she asked him plainly. Her boldness took Harry by surprise.

"Yes," said Harry. "How did you—"

"You've been here a while now. People find out. We're not as stupid as Franklin thinks we are. I'm Bernadette O'Connor." She offered her hand. Harry shook it.

"Hi. My name is Harry Drewes." The skin on her hand felt tough and hard, like leather. Not at all like the hands of the young women he knew in New York.

"You're going to be all right," she told him. "You took in a good amount of the dust. If you're not used to it, it can hurt you bad."

Several other people seemed to gain the confidence to come forward, too. They made a half circle around Harry and looked down at him.

Harry saw how tired and worn their faces were. It was hard to tell just how old they might be.

"I'm feeling much better," he told them.

"That's because you had a mask on," she suggested.

"Yes," said Harry. "Why don't all of you wear masks?"

The people standing over Harry sneered. "Yeah, Bernadette, how come we don't?" a few of them asked in mock wonder.

Bernadette gave Harry a kind smile. She said simply, "I think you'd better ask Mr. Franklin about that."

"Or your mother," said another voice from the crowd. Then a large man with a scruffy beard stepped from the crowd. His face was hard and dark. A front tooth was missing and his right eye was swollen.

"Go ahead," he said. "Ask your mother why the workers don't wear masks. She'll tell you they ain't worth it, that's why. Workers are no better than animals."

Some of the others grumbled. Harry couldn't tell if they were agreeing or disagreeing with the man.

"He doesn't make the rules, Nick," said Bernadette.

"No," the man snarled. "But he has a rich life because of them. That much is true."

Once more the people grumbled. This time, Harry knew they were in agreement.

"What I wouldn't give for half of what this kid had for breakfast this morning," someone said. The others laughed and nodded.

"I bet it could feed my whole family for a week," another moaned.

"A month!" another replied with a sneer. As the crowd grew louder and angrier, Bernadette jumped onto a bench.

She cried, "Listen to you! You're all crying like a bunch of babies. Picking on this lad isn't going to change your lot. This is what I've been preaching to you all along.

"Growling won't help. You moan and you cuss at your wives, husbands, and kids. You tell them how terrible your life is and how you hate it in this prison of a work place. That makes you feel better. You get all nice and warm and cozy inside because you've let out your anger. But you haven't gained anything, or changed anything. You just made your home life worse. The job stays the same."

"Tell them, Bernadette!" a voice shouted.

But someone else said, "Keep it down, Bernadette. You want Franklin to hear you?"

"Yes," she said angrily. "He does hear already. But someone's got to make him *listen*. If you want change, you have to demand it. If you don't, things will go on the way they always have. So stop kicking your dogs and start fighting where it counts."

The workers cheered and clapped their hands. Then Harry heard a shrill whistle. Everyone looked over to their left. A little man in a newsboy cap was waving a red hankie. Harry knew it was some sort of signal.

The crowd of workers began to split up. They walked away just as Carl and Josh turned the corner. Nick helped Bernadette down from the bench.

Harry saw the angry look on Carl's face. He stared at the workers as they walked back into the mill and then looked over at Bernadette and Nick.

Nick bent down and whispered to Harry. "You tell Franklin and his bodyguard anything about this, boy, and you and I will have a little chat."

"Oh shut up," said Bernadette. "Let him say what he likes."

She turned to Harry and smiled once more. "You're welcome at the mill anytime," she said. "You have a right to be here, too. No one here really blames you. If they do, then they're wrong."

Harry had never met a woman with so much spirit and life. She seemed unafraid and strong. This woman was not like the young ladies he had known in the city. They were all lace and silk. All secret looks and glances. Bernadette seemed fearless.

She let out a friendly laugh and backed away. But she backed right into Josh. She turned and saw the giant man staring down at her.

"Why, hello Josh," she said. "Fancy running into you," she added smiling.

Carl turned to Harry and said, "I see you met the O'Connors. I thought I heard some cheering. Speaking in public again, are we Bernadette?"

"No," said Harry quickly. "She was just welcoming me. She made a nice speech and the others applauded."

"How nice of her. She often says things that make the others applaud and cheer," Carl told him.

Nick said, "She's got a gift—a gift for getting people excited." Then Nick looked right at Carl and said, "And when people get excited, they can do some amazing things."

Nick and Carl glared at one another. Harry did not know what was going on between them. But whatever it was, it frightened him. The two men seemed as though they were trying to kill one another with angry looks.

"Just get back to work," Carl snapped. "I don't pay you two to make speeches. I pay you to make paper. Now get going!"

Bernadette started to walk back to the mill but Nick stood firm against Carl.

Bernadette called back in warning, "Come on, Nick."

Nick stood his ground. Then Josh took a step forward. Carl said to Nick, "After last week, I'd have thought you'd be a little more willing to do as I ask."

Harry looked at Nick's face. Had he been beaten up by Josh? Whatever had happened between them, Nick did not seem bothered by it now.

At last Bernadette grabbed Nick by the arm and said, "Let's go!"

"Best listen to your sister, Nick," Carl told him. "She is indeed a smart woman."

Finally Nick backed down and headed for the mill.

Harry breathed a little easier. The standoff had surprised him. He had no idea there was such trouble here. If only he could walk freely between Carl and the workers. If only he could come and go in both their worlds. He could learn so much!

Walking back to Carl's office Harry said, "I didn't realize things were so tense here."

Carl was still angry from the scene with Nick. He snapped, "What do you mean, tense? Why that was just a little problem— nothing that me and Josh can't handle. Don't you go telling your momma that things are boiling around here."

"I didn't mean it like that," Harry said. "I know workers and managers don't always get along. It's just that—"

"Me and the workers, we get on fine," Carl said. "And that's a fact. It's just that those O'Connors are born troublemakers. They stir everybody up. They get 'em all worked up and hot!"

Harry decided it was best to say no

more. But he had to laugh to himself. Carl was a lot like Harry's Grandfather Jefferson. Once he got going, there was no stopping him. There was no sense arguing with a man like that.

"Now," said Carl, "If you're here to learn the business, I can teach you plenty. I'll show you about working payroll. Then we can go over organizing the shifts. But you won't learn anything dwelling on scenes like that one. Sorry you had to see that at all. We got a peaceful community here. We run a tight ship, too."

"I know you do," Harry replied as they reached Carl's office.

"Well then . . ." Carl walked over to the bookshelf. He took out three large leather volumes.

Harry frowned. He did not like the thought of spending the next few hours with dusty old books. Harry had made a deal with Olive, his mother, to stay at the mill all summer. There would be plenty of time for looking at the books later.

"You know," Harry said, "I think I'd just like to have a walk first. Get some fresh air before I start."

"Suit yourself," said Carl with a shrug. "Just keep out of the way of the O'Connors. And watch yourself around the machinery. The last thing I need is for you to hurt yourself. Your mother would have my hide."

"Don't worry," said Harry. "I'll be fine. I promise."

Harry was glad to get away from Carl's fussing, and he was happy to hide from Josh's watchful eye. Josh made him nervous.

After Harry left Carl's office he saw Bernadette sitting in a hallway. She was sitting with an older woman whose hand was bleeding. Bernadette was wrapping a rag around the woman's fingers.

"Is she all right?" asked Harry.

Bernadette nodded, but said nothing.

"Can I get Mr. Franklin?"

"No," said the woman quickly. "Leave him out of this. We can manage fine without him . . . or you."

Bernadette smiled at Harry and eased the tension. "This is Sarah. I'm taking care of her just fine."

"Then at least let me get you the doctor," Harry said.

"Doctor," Sarah said. "Hah!"

"There is no doctor or nurse at the mill," Bernadette replied. "There's one in town. But that would mean taking the day off to see him. And that would mean Sarah loses a day's pay. The doctor might even tell her to stop work for a while. No one can afford to do that."

"Save your voice for the town hall tonight," said Sarah.

"No doctor?" asked Harry. He was amazed. There were nurses at all the family's mills and factories back East. Some even had doctors on call.

"We had a doctor," Bernadette said. "Then Mr. Franklin got rid of him. Cost too much, he said. The doctor made too many demands. He wanted the sick and hurt to stay away from work. Franklin didn't like that. So the doctor didn't last long."

Sarah looked cautiously around the hall. "I'd best get back inside," she said. "If the floor boss catches me I'll be out for sure."

"This is silly," said Harry. "You act as though this is some sort of prison. Surely things can't be that bad."

"You're a young man," said Bernadette. "You have a lot to learn. Why are you here anyway?"

Harry helped Bernadette to her feet and walked her down the hall. He said, "I wanted to go West. To see life and be on my own. My mother wanted me to stay home and learn the business. So this trip was a kind of middle ground. I'm here to learn the business from Carl—and whatever I can from life."

"Well," said Bernadette, "you came to a fine place to learn about life. The people here are real and good. But as for learning anything from Mr. Carl Franklin, heaven help you."

"Does everyone feel the way you do about him?"

"Everyone who dares to feel anything anymore. Everyone who hasn't given up hope."

"You seem to give them hope," said Harry.

"Yes—I do. But I want to give them more than that. So I preach to them any chance I can. I tell them they don't have to be victims of Carl Franklin.

"Not all managers are bad," Bernadette

went on. "Not all mill owners are bad. There are good places to work, I figure. Why not make it good here?

"People need to stand up, to fight back," she said. "I want to see they get what's fair, that's all. And if you want to learn something of life, remember this: Treat people fairly and make sure they treat you the same way. That's what I believe."

Bernadette and Harry walked down the hall to large double doors. Harry heard the noisy rumblings of the machines. He could see the haze of the dust in the air.

"I've got to get back to work," she said.

"Will Sarah be all right?" asked Harry.

She nodded yes.

"What did she mean, 'save your voice for the town hall'?"

Bernadette looked around cautiously. "The others would tar and feather me if they knew I told you. But I think you're a good man. We're having a meeting at the town hall tonight.

"I'm going to burn their ears," she said with a twinkle in her eyes. "I'm going to stir them up something fine. And get them to see that they have rights in the work place."

Bernadette moved to open the giant double doors. She stopped and turned to Harry. She said, "I'm counting on you to keep that to yourself, young man."

Harry promised he would. He watched her as she disappeared behind the door into the haze-filled room.

Harry turned from the doors and saw Josh. The big man half-smiled at Harry and walked around a corner. Harry wondered how much he had heard.

4

That night after dinner, Harry asked Carl for a ride into town. He wanted a chance to get out and hear Bernadette speak.

"What do you want in town?" asked Carl.

"Oh, just to look around and see the sights. I haven't yet seen the town at *night*."

"The sights of Redfield?" Carl laughed. "There are just a few saloons, a bank and a blacksmith—nothing for you to bother with. Besides, the town at night is no place for a decent young man. After sunset the workers from the mill turn it into a wild west town. All they do is drink and fight. And waste their money."

Harry felt like a prisoner. Carl seemed to think he was babysitting "Olive's little boy." Harry was missing out on the very thing he came west to see—life and people!

"All I want to do is go into town for a little while," Harry pleaded. "I've been here for weeks."

"As long as you're in my care, Harry, I promised your mother I'd look after you. Besides, this isn't a good night for it."

"What do you mean?" asked Harry.

"It just isn't," Carl replied, as if he expected the conversation to end then and there.

Harry wondered if Carl knew anything about Bernadette speaking at the town hall. He was too afraid to ask.

"Now, you'd best get yourself on upstairs and review those records I showed you," Carl went on. "If you expect to manage a place like this one someday, it's a chore you'll need to get used to."

Harry rose from his chair and grabbed the record books roughly. He shoved them under his arm and stormed out of the room.

Harry had been away from home for weeks. But he still felt he hadn't seen much. The workers he'd met at the mill seemed to be honest people—hard working and hard living. But he never managed to see them outside of work. What were their dreams and their goals? What did they want out of life?

Harry set Carl's log books aside. He was not about to read another ledger tonight.

Harry waited an hour until Carl came upstairs. It was nearly 10:30 P.M. Carl came to knock on Harry's door. As usual, he asked if Harry was all right. Harry said he was fine and was going to bed.

When he heard Carl close his bedroom door, Harry threw on a jacket, picked up his shoes, and tiptoed down the back stairway. The old house seemed to creak with every step he took.

Finally Harry reached the bottom of the stairs and crept out the back door. He sat on the back porch steps and put on his shoes. The night was as dark as tar. No moon shone. He carefully made his way to the barn.

When Harry reached the barn, he opened the doors and saw that the buggy was gone. The barn was empty.

Suddenly he heard the loud crack of a whip. Horses whinnied and wood rattled against metal. Then two black horses appeared like ghosts. When they galloped into the light of the house, Harry saw the buggy. Josh was driving the horses right toward him. Harry stepped aside and watched the buggy slow down, then come to rest within a few feet of the barn.

Harry saw Carl's light on. He took hold of the horses' reins to calm them.

"What you doin' out here, boy?" snarled Josh.

"I could ask you the same thing," Harry replied fearlessly. He saw that Josh was clutching his side as he climbed down from the buggy.

Just then Carl came rushing out of the house. He spied Josh and then Harry. He looked more surprised to see Harry.

"What the devil is going on?" he shouted.

"I was just out for a stroll when I heard the noise," Harry said.

Josh stumbled toward the house and he glanced over at Harry. He looked guilty. Harry couldn't understand what was going on.

"Well don't just stand there boy," Carl shouted at Harry. "Make yourself useful. Put the buggy away."

Carl helped Josh into the house. Harry was confused. Why was Josh out so late? Harry felt lucky that he had not been caught taking the buggy. He climbed aboard and sat on the leather seat. Something shiny was reflected in the light coming from the kitchen. Harry touched it, and saw it was a puddle.

"Blood," he whispered to himself.

He looked into the kitchen. Inside, he saw Carl standing over Josh and shouting at him. Harry strained to hear, but he couldn't make out a word.

Harry checked the reins and found them wet with more blood. The whole cab, in fact, was splattered with blood.

Suddenly the night seemed darker than Harry could stand. Now he wanted nothing more than to get the buggy safely in the barn and get back indoors.

Once inside the house, Harry saw that his hands and clothes were stained with blood. What's more, the kitchen chair was also bloodied. Harry had seen Josh sitting there just minutes ago. The maid, dressed in a robe and house slippers, scurried into the kitchen.

"Is Josh all right?" Harry asked her.

"He'll be fine," she said. "Just clean yourself off outside and I'll take care of the mess in here."

"What happened to him?" asked Harry.

The maid shook her head and shooed him away. "If you know what's good for you, you'll just get yourself upstairs to bed. And don't ask any more questions."

Harry walked outside to the water pump. The night was quiet now. The horses were silent. Carl had stopped his shouting. The maid was no longer complaining about the mess.

In the distance an owl hooted sadly. The lonesome sound sent shivers up Harry's spine. He washed the blood off his hands. And he tried to get the blood out of his pants and shirt. But somehow it wouldn't wash away.

CHAPTER

5

When he woke up the next morning, Harry hoped the whole episode had been a terrible dream. Outside, the sky was blue, the weather was warm, and birds chirped in the trees. Maybe it had just been a nightmare after all.

But then Harry looked over at his clothes. He saw they were still stained a deep red.

Then Harry heard the angry voices chanting. At first the sound was like a murmur, but it soon grew louder.

Harry bolted from his bed. He ran to the window and looked down the road. He saw a group of people marching toward the house. Harry thought there must be around fifty of them—all men. As they marched closer, Harry could see that they carried clubs, bats, and pipes.

Suddenly the bedroom door flew open, banging against the wall, and chipping away some of the paint. Carl stood on the threshold.

"Stay in your room, lad," Carl said. "Just stay where you are. Everything will be all right."

Carl carried a shotgun. He checked its chambers and then stormed downstairs.

What was happening? Harry wished he knew. He was sure of just one thing—whatever happened to Josh last night had something to do with the problem this morning.

Harry threw on some clothes and sat at the window. He could see that Nick was the man leading the pack. He also saw that Bernadette's brother was crazed with anger.

The group of men shouted and raised their clubs in the air. They smashed down Carl's white picket gate and marched onto his neatly groomed lawn. Nick raised his arms high into the air and signaled the men to stop. Suddenly the crowd grew quiet.

Nick shouted, "Franklin! You and your thug Josh McKinley get out here!" Then he added, "Now!"

The other men grew bolder. They shouted and jeered all the more.

Carl Franklin walked calmly out of the house, carrying his shotgun. He stood silently before the angry crowd and listened to them whoop, and holler. Then he raised his rifle into the air and shot off a deafening blast.

The sound echoed all the way down the valley. Some of the men stopped their shouting and some backed off a step. But Nick stood his ground.

Carl looked Nick right in the eyes. "You'd best have a mighty good reason to destroy a man's property and put the fear of God into his houseguest," he said. "I don't take kindly to drunken toughs."

"One rifle won't stop all of us, Franklin," said Nick. Harry could see the hate in Nick's eyes. He looked like a man who was ready to fight—to the death.

"Well, it'll stop *one* of you," Carl said. "Who wants to be the one?"

No one spoke.

"I didn't think so," said Carl. "Now why don't you all calm down. Tell me why a bunch of healthy men choose to stay away from the mill. You all find other work?"

Nick snapped, "You'll find the answer to that question at the bottom of Clary Hill. That's where we found my sister this morning."

His sister, thought Harry. He means Bernadette. But what does he mean, "where we *found*" her?"

Harry watched as Carl slowly lowered his rifle. "What happened?" he asked.

"We have our suspicions. We found Bernadette's body at the bottom of the hill. She was crushed to death when her buggy and her mule went over."

"I'm sorry to hear that," said Carl. But as soon as he spoke, the men began to grumble again. It was obvious to Harry that they didn't believe him. Harry wondered whether they should.

"I don't like to see any of my people hurt," Carl went on.

"What do you mean?" snarled Nick. "You hated her. You knew she could stir the workers up with her talk. You cut her wages, and made her work longer hours. But that didn't stop her."

"All right," said Carl, "listen to me. I'm just trying to run this mill as best I know how. I'm not the one caused your sister's death. Sounds like an act of God to me."

"Act of God?" several men shouted. They moved even closer to Carl. They were ready to strike. Carl raised his gun once more.

"Now if you get back to work, I might be willing to forget all about this," Carl said.

Then Harry saw Nick throw down his club and slowly walk up the porch stairs. He stood head to head with Carl. Carl put his finger on the trigger, ready for any sudden move.

"I ain't here to argue with you, Franklin," Nick growled. "I'm here to tell you. There were two sets of tracks on the hill where Bernadette's buggy went over. Someone else was there, all right.

"Now I'm sure you were safe and sound in that big bed of yours," Nick continued. "But your handyman, Josh, was seen at the town hall last night. He was there when Bernadette spoke to us. And he left about the same time she did. All we want is Josh."

The other men shouted their agreement.

"He's not here," Carl shouted back. "I don't keep track of Josh anymore than I keep track of you. You find him, you can talk to him."

Someone shouted, "Take him, Nick. Take Franklin till we can find Josh." Some of the others agreed.

"I say we rip the house apart," another man said. "He's hiding in there somewhere!" Several men roared their approval.

Nick turned on them and spoke. "No!" he shouted back. "That's just what Franklin wants us to do. If we go into his house, he'll get the police on us."

Then Harry watched as Nick turned back to Carl and spoke in a slow, clear voice. "I was hoping we could talk this through," he said. "I know why my sister was killed. And I think you know who did it. Well, I aim to hit you where it hurts." He addressed the men behind him.

"Men," he called, "you heard Bernadette last night. You heard what she had to say. She told us we could have a better life. She told us we should band together and demand what's fair. She called on us to strike. And I say we do just that."

The men cheered and clapped their hands. They hooted and hollered, but Carl stood firm. He fired another shot into the air.

"You'll starve before you see an extra cent," he shouted. "I have men who'll work in your place."

"I don't think so," Nick replied. "Every man, woman, and child is with us. You won't see a soul there tomorrow. That's a lot of jobs to fill."

Nick led the men off Carl's property. They trampled his fence and bushes before they marched back down the street, chanting and whooping.

Harry saw Carl running after them. He waved his fist into the air and shouted, "There are ways to solve your problems! I don't take to blackmail. You're a fool, Nick O'Connor! I'll see you behind bars!"

Carl cussed and kicked the fence. He flung his rifle toward the house. "I'll not be threatened!" he yelled. "Not by any man!"

Harry ran downstairs. He called to Carl. "Are you all right?" he asked.

"The fools," was all he could say in reply. "I'll crush them. Don't they know that?"

Carl stormed past Harry and went back inside the house. Harry tried his best to pick up bits and pieces of the fence. He put them in a pile. He placed the wooden gate by the porch stairs.

He didn't know what else to do. He didn't want to go back inside, so he walked to the barn to inspect the buggy. He was surprised to see that it was gone.

"Josh!" Harry said to himself. "He's gone." He figured Josh must have taken the buggy and left during the night.

Harry walked back to his room and wrote in his journal:

"I've always said I wanted to see life. Now I don't know what I really meant by that. I've hated the way Carl has pampered and sheltered me here—just like mother had at home. Now, suddenly, the world has come crashing in on me. Is this what "life" is? It is angrier and uglier than I would have ever thought possible.

"I've said that all I wanted was just to observe life. To watch. But how long can I sit back and just look on like it is some kind of play?"

As if in answer to this question, Carl burst into his room. He seemed a bit calmer now, and more serious.

"What are you writing?" Carl asked.

"My journal," said Harry, closing his book quickly.

"You wouldn't be writing to your mother, would you?"

"No."

"Good. I'll tell her everything that happened in good time. There's no sense in upsetting her now. Besides, this fuss will blow over soon."

"Will it?" Harry asked with doubt in his voice. "We'll have to tell her sometime soon. I know Mother and I know that—"

"You jut do as I say for now. I want you to go into town."

"The buggy's gone," Harry replied.

"Never mind that," said Carl. "You're a strong young man. The walk will do you good. It'll take you no more than an hour to get there."

Carl sat beside Harry. "This is your chance to prove yourself Harry," Carl said. "I need your help."

"What can I do?" Harry asked.

"I want you to go into town. Put on a hat and cloak. No one will notice you. I want you to get within a half mile of the mill. I want you to tell me what's going on there."

Harry started to protest. "Surely the police will—"

"The police have other plans for now. This is not a big town. There are not many police. Some of them will be nearby. But I need you to report to me, to tell me what the workers are planning."

"But if they see me—"

"They won't. And even if they do, they'll never harm you."

"But—"

Carl stood and walked to the door. He wasn't listening. He was about to leave when Harry stopped him.

"Carl," Harry said. "What happened last night?" Carl did not reply. Harry said, "When I put the buggy away, I found blood all over the seat and more in the kitchen where Josh sat. What happened last night? I want to know."

"That's none of your worry," Carl snapped.

"It certainly is!" Harry answered sharply as he stood and moved to Carl. "I met Bernadette. I talked with her. She was a good woman. Last night she died. And last night, Josh came back hurt and bleeding. What did he do? And where is he now?"

Harry stood firm, but so did the older man. Carl said, "Harry! As long as you are under this roof, you'll do as I say. And I say, go into town."

"I don't want to take sides in this," Harry said. "This is not my—"

Carl let out a snarling laugh. "Take sides! My boy, you chose your side the day you put on those fancy clothes of yours. You chose sides the day you sat at my table and ate my food. The day you were born a Drewes, you took sides. It's a matter of loyalty. Report back to me tonight!"

Carl walked out and slammed the door shut. Harry knew that he could no longer just sit and watch life go by. Carl was right—he had chosen. It was a matter of loyalty. And that loyalty was being put to a test.

Harry went into town and saw the strikers. As he had feared, Nick meant everything he had told Carl. Harry was sure there would be trouble now. There was no way to avoid it.

He wished he could smooth things over. A part of him felt that he could do it, too. If only he could talk to Nick, and if he could just reason with Carl! But it was too late for that. The strike was on.

Back at Carl's house that night, Harry wrote in his journal:

"Nick and his men have set up camp near the mill. They are being joined by hundreds of other mill workers.

"Some of them are afraid that strike breakers and police will come to attack them during the night. Others worry that they will be thrown out of their homes.

"After all, it is the mill that feeds and clothes them. The mill puts roofs over their heads. If they stay away from work too long, Mr. Franklin would have their homes boarded up. But I can't believe he would do such a thing."

Within a few days, Nick and his followers got ready for anything. They set up more tents and brought in beds and stoves. Now, even if Carl did take their homes away, they would be prepared.

For two weeks they held on. For two weeks they stood as one community. Police rode by daily and threatened them. But Nick and his men stood firm.

Carl had found a few people to take up the work. But not enough. Soon the mill had to shut down.

Harry watched Carl and wondered how long he would put up with it. Every day he grew more and more quiet. He hardly talked at all any more, even to yell and scold.

Harry tried to feel sorry for him, but he could not. He believed Carl had basically been a good man—once. But he seemed to have lost his reason and any sense of fairness. In the last week, he'd had the workers' houses boarded up.

Then, there was still the question of Bernadette's death. Every night Harry lay awake and wondered what really happened to Bernadette on Clary Hill.

Had she died in an accident? Had Josh killed her and somehow hurt himself as well? Harry realized he might never know for certain. But as each day passed, he grew more uncomfortable with Carl. After a while Harry began to suspect Carl of causing the whole mess. Maybe Carl did not tell Josh to hurt Bernadette—but he had helped Josh to escape. He was hiding something.

"Harry!" Carl called one morning.

Harry came downstairs. He looked at Carl coldly. "What do you want?" he asked.

To Harry's surprise, Carl was in a better mood today. He seemed brighter and happier. "This is no place for a young man like you," he said. "I have a ticket for you on the first train leaving Redfield tomorrow for New York."

"That's fine with me," said Harry. "I haven't been any help to you anyway."

Carl stood and looked Harry in the eyes. "You don't like me much, do you, boy?"

"Not really," said Harry. "It seems to me the workers don't ask for much. They ask to be looked after when they get hurt. They ask for better conditions in the mill. They ask for shorter days—"

"And you don't think those demands amount to much, eh?"

Harry shook his head.

"Well, the way I see it, all that will be over tomorrow night," Carl said.

Harry's eyes narrowed with suspicion. "What happens tomorrow night?" he asked.

Carl sat back down in his rocker. He took out a big cigar and lit it.

"How long do you think it would be before the strikers started hurting *you*?" Carl began, changing the subject.

"Me?"

"I don't mean physically. I mean in the pocketbook. A month? Two months? Then your momma would have to close this mill. Maybe shut down another factory. Soon, you'd be wearing rags instead of those fancy duds you wear now.

"How much," he continued, "would you be willing to give those workers from your own pocket? If it was *your* money—how many nurses would you hire? How many improvements would you make?"

"I'd do whatever I needed to. At least I hope I would," replied Harry.

"Suppose for every extra penny that you gave them, you also had to give something else up? What then?"

"What do you mean?"

"You give them a penny *and* you have to give up all your nice clothes—"

"That's silly," Harry said.

"Another penny for them means no more fancy New York apartment for you. Another penny and no more nice books. You think you'd still care then? You think you'd still worry yourself to sleep at night?"

"What's your point?" asked Harry.

"My point is that *I'm* the one who's putting my life on the line. I'm only trying to keep your momma's business from going under. And if that means waiting out those lazy ruffians, I'll do it. And if that means hiring men to . . ." Carl stopped short.

"To what?" asked Harry.

"The workers are breaking the law, son."

"What happens tomorrow night?" Harry asked. "What are you going to do?"

"I need to keep that mill open. It's my job. It's what I've been hired to do! Now you'd best pack your things."

"Get me out of the way before the trouble begins, right?" Harry said. "What are you going to do? Bring back Josh? Bring back ten more Joshes? Do to the others what he did to Bernadette?"

"That's enough," shouted Carl. "I'll bring in as many men as I need. And there will be plenty of them—you can count on that."

"Armed?" asked Harry.

Carl did not reply. He just sat there staring out the window, smoking his cigar.

Harry said, "If you think you're doing this to please my mother, you're wrong. She would never agree to bring in toughs and thugs. I'll tell her about this. Either way, Mr. Franklin, . . . you're through."

Carl blew a stream of smoke toward the ceiling. He smiled. "I don't think so. Your mother told me to do whatever I needed to do."

He handed Harry a telegram. Harry read it. It said that Carl should handle the strike in whatever way he thought best.

Harry threw down the telegram. "She doesn't know you're planning *this*. If you bring in armed men, there'll be a massacre."

"Your momma said, 'whatever.'"

"Anyway, I've written her about all this," Harry said coolly. "Once she knows the facts, I'm certain she'll see things differently."

Carl stood. The conversation was over. "The mail here is not like it is in New York," he said, smiling. "It tends to be slower in Oregon. Sometimes, it even gets lost."

Harry couldn't believe his ears. Had Carl actually taken his letters and not sent them home?

"I haven't heard from Mother since the strike began," Harry said, almost to himself. "You took my letters! You destroyed them! My mother—"

"Your mother doesn't have to live with these people, or keep them in line. This is *my* mill. These are my people. They work by my rules. I've made a name for myself in this town. I'll be mayor in another year. I'll own this town."

"So, that's what all this means to you—power. You don't care about the workers or my family, do you? This is your little kingdom and you're the mighty ruler."

"Train leaves at 7:00 A.M.," Carl replied. "It's for your own good, boy."

7

At midnight, Harry sneaked down the backstairs. He took only his and Hattie's journals with him. All his clothes and his books he left behind.

Before turning the lights out, he had written:

"Mr. Franklin said I had chosen sides the minute I was born. I do not agree. We have choices all our lives. No one is born into one single way of life. And no one is born into one single way of thinking. I don't have to be on the side of either the poor or the rich. I don't have to be on the side of the mill worker or the mill owner. I am on the side of truth and fairness. I will join whoever is right against whatever is wrong. I will join whoever is just against whoever seeks to crush justice. That is my choice. Tonight, I have made my choice."

In the darkness, Harry began his trip toward town. A little more than an hour later, he saw the mill. The sight of it at night was overpowering. It loomed out of the darkness like a sleeping giant. It looked huge and mighty.

He saw the tents on some land near the mill. The camp looked like a small city. Here and there fires were burning. People stood near the fires warming themselves. Harry could barely make out the faces of the mothers, children, old men, and young boys. But he heard many of them singing—*singing* of all things! And someone was playing a fiddle.

Most of the people just sat and waited. Some men watched. Harry figured they were waiting for trouble. He only hoped they were ready for it.

Harry walked closer and closer to the strikers.

"Halt!" someone cried. "Who is it?"

"Harry Drewes. I've come to give a message to Nick."

"That's the owner's kid," someone called out.

"Go back to your mommy—boy!" another cried out.

"I have an important message," Harry said. "Please!"

"We don't deal with messenger boys. If Franklin wants to talk let him come here himself."

Then Harry heard a familiar voice. It was Nick. "Let him come on," he growled.

The guard let Harry through.

"What do you want to tell me?" said Nick. "It must be something big. You're risking your life coming here. A few days ago I might have taken you hostage."

Harry said, "Can I talk to you in private?"

"We don't have secrets here," said Nick. "You tell me and you tell us all."

Harry looked around at the people walking toward him. He could feel their fear and their anger as they formed a circle around him. It made him very nervous.

"Mr. Franklin . . . he plans to call out men to storm your community."

The crowd stirred.

"How many men?" asked Nick.

"I'm not sure," Harry answered. "He said as many as he needed. He plans to attack the tents tomorrow night. They'll have guns I'm sure. And they mean to crush you all."

The crowd began chattering. Some women began to cry and some men cursed. Some ran to warn the others and some ran to get their weapons. But Nick stood firm.

"You believe the kid?" someone asked Nick.

Nick looked Harry right in the eyes. He stared at him for a moment, and then he said, "Yes, I do. Bernadette was a good judge of people. She took a liking to this fellow. It's Carl Franklin I don't believe. When did Franklin tell you this?" Nick asked.

"Just this evening," said Harry. "I sneaked out as soon as I could."

"And he made a point of telling you that they would attack *tomorrow* night?"

"Yes," Harry answered.

"Does he usually tell you things? Secrets like this?"

Harry thought about that for a moment. Carl had said almost nothing to him for two weeks. He had hardly said a word to Harry until tonight.

"No," Harry said. "He doesn't usually tell me much."

"Then it makes sense. We're in more trouble than even *you* thought, Harry. Though you may have saved many a life."

Nick turned to the others and said, "Franklin and his men are going to fight for the mill—tonight!"

"What?" Harry said. "Are you sure, Nick?"

Nick grabbed Harry by the shoulders and said, "Franklin was counting on you coming here to tell us this. He figured we'd sit around all night and plan for the *next* day. But we'll be ready for him!"

Nick jumped upon a wooden table and shouted at the crowd of people.

"Listen to me, all of you! All we've asked Franklin to give us is fair and honest treatment. You know that. Bernadette knew it, too. But Carl Franklin is not an honest man. Tonight he plans to take this little town by force. He plans to let us know who is in power and who isn't. Well, we'll be ready!"

The crowd let out a roar. As they were shouting, Nick stepped down and gathered a few of his men around him.

Softly he said, "This is going to be an all out battle. I know it. Get all the women and children over into the woods. Then I want every man with a hunting rifle to get it and come back here. Anyone who wants out had better leave now." No one moved.

"Then we're all in this together," said Nick.

The men began to move quickly. Within an hour, all the women and children were safely away from the camp. The men had taken every bit of furniture from the tents. They grabbed every piece of equipment they owned. They piled them up and used them as barriers.

Harry pitched in where he could. He had never fired a gun before. He didn't want to, either. But he helped the women and children get away. And he helped the men strengthen their barricades.

As he gave orders, Nick helped like everyone else. He carried weapons and drove buggies. In a few hours, Nick and the others had made the tent city as strong as it could be.

Then there was nothing to do but wait. Each man, stared into the darkness, waiting. They heard sounds every second— sounds like car engines and horses' hooves and voices. But they were just noises. Nothing happened.

The night wore on. Nick began to wonder if, in fact, Harry had been told the truth. In another hour or so it would be dawn. Some of the men had even fallen asleep.

Then the roar of an engine awoke them. It was an awful sound of metal grinding against metal. It hissed and spit like a giant steam engine. It roared like an old boiler.

"What the devil is that?" someone whispered.

The noise grew louder. Then they heard the horses' hooves. There was no mistaking the sound this time. It was the dull thunder of hooves.

"Must be a hundred of them, maybe more," Nick said.

Harry's stomach churned. He felt sure he was going to die—he could feel it in his gut. He closed his eyes and uttered a prayer. Maybe things would be all right.

The growl of the engine turned into a horrible scream. The men could see headlights like fiery dragon eyes, burning through the night.

"Get ready!" shouted Nick.

Ready for what, Harry thought. What was it? It looked like some kind of tank.

They could see the horses now. There were about 50 of them clearly visible. A row of men with clubs and rifles marched ahead of them.

Even before a shot was fired, women and children began crying. Men began to sweat and shake and a few ran away.

Harry thought about running, too. He didn't know what kept him from doing it. There he was, clutching a gun he had never fired before, fighting a fight that was not really his own. He was afraid. He tried to pray again but nothing came. His mind was blank.

The armed men advanced, but they didn't fire. Harry wondered what they were waiting for. Why don't they just get it over with?

Wildly, he wondered if the armed men had been sent as a show of force. Maybe they would simply threaten. Maybe this whole mess could be avoided.

Harry had almost convinced himself of that when a hail of bullets exploded from the dragon—the armored car. As the car rolled into the camp, men scattered everywhere.

"Hold your ground!" shouted Nick. "Stay where you are. They're trying to draw your fire."

It was true. The bullets had been fired over the strikers' heads. But the trick had worked. Nick's men began to fire back and leave their cover. They ran in all directions to wherever they thought were safer spots.

It looked like a hurricane of confusion was whirling through the tent city. The armored car spit more bullets and the men on horseback charged. The rest of Franklin's men rushed into the camp with torches, rifles, and clubs.

The noise was horrible. Harry picked up his gun and began to fire. He couldn't see, but he just kept firing.

Franklin's men began tossing torches into the tents. Fires sprang up almost immediately, sending people running everywhere. The men on horseback leapt over the tables, chairs, and buggies, firing at random.

Whatever order Nick had imposed on his men was gone now. Everyone was shooting without purpose. All around him,

Harry saw dying men screaming for help. The fires were burning out of control. It seemed as though the entire tent city was ablaze. The heat was horrible.

The armored car ripped through the city, turned and came directly toward Nick and his men. Harry jumped and pointed toward the car. He grabbed Nick by the shoulder.

"Nick," he cried. "It's coming this way!"

Before his words faded into the air, the car spit out another hail of bullets. More men scattered, but Harry and Nick stood their ground. Only six men were left beside them—the others had been killed or had run off.

Nick signaled for the men to fall back as the armored car came closer. Harry and the others did as Nick ordered. They fell back and hid behind a row of plows and tables.

But Nick did not follow them. He stood fast and fired at the car. He just kept shooting. When he ran out of bullets he reloaded and shot again.

"Get back!" cried Harry. But Nick wouldn't listen.

The armored car fired again and again. The bullets ripped the dust and grass around Nick. Harry heard the hissing and then he heard three short thuds. Nick was hurled backwards. He staggered, then tried to get to his feet.

Harry saw that Nick had been badly hit. "They'll kill him," shouted Harry as he rushed from behind a plow. As he ran toward Nick, the car rolled closer.

Harry grabbed Nick and he began to drag him toward cover. Bullets whizzed by their heads. Harry fell to his knees. He clutched Nick by the neck and shoulder. Together they crawled nearer the barricades.

But the car was too quick for them and the men inside the car were too eager. More bullets exploded all around them. Then Harry heard another thud, and another. He felt Nick go completely limp in his arms.

The car rolled onward, racing by Harry as though the men inside it had never even seen him. Nick lay still in Harry's arms. Harry realized he was dead.

Harry saw the tents ablaze and bodies scattered all over the ground. There must be a hundred people dead or wounded here, thought Harry.

At last, the gunfire stopped. Men still ran and horses still jumped and reared. But the horrible sound of gunfire had stopped.

There was no need to shoot anymore. The battle had ended almost as soon as it had started. Nick's ragtag workers were no match for the armed men of Carl Franklin.

The armored car drove off. The horses' hooves pounded and clip-clopped away. Only a few dozen armed guards still walked about. Now and then Harry could hear a woman scream or a man cry out in pain. And he could hear the children crying all around him.

Suddenly Harry felt weak and lightheaded. His chest began to hurt and his heart began to pound. He looked down and saw that he was bleeding. He thought the blood was from Nick's wounds. But then he looked again and saw the rip in his jacket. He saw the blood oozing through his shirt. "I've been hit," he said aloud.

He staggered back to the place where he had hidden his journals. He wanted to write an entry—a note to his mother. He had to write one last note explaining things, one last note to tell her he loved her. But he hadn't the strength.

The tent city seemed to whirl around him. The blazing fires roared and hissed and he began to sweat. Then he felt chills.

He picked up Hattie's journal and opened it. How often it had given him comfort, and helped him through dark times. Maybe he could read one last page. Yes, that would make him feel better.

Harry looked toward the east and saw that the sun was rising. A new day was beginning. The last thing Harry Drewes saw was the sun breaking over the hills, it's rays thrusting long slivers of light into the valley.

He did not want to give up yet. He wanted to see this nightmare through to the end. He wanted to see the workers get what they asked for. Harry knew that Carl's days of managing the mill were over. Carl had dug his own grave. No matter what happened now, his family would get rid of Franklin. Harry told himself that the workers would get a better man. He told himself that from now on conditions would be better, safer. But what a terrible price had been paid. Dozens were dead—maybe more. Entire families had been destroyed. And all out of suspicion and fear.

When his mother found him, Harry was still clutching Hattie's journal. He was laying face down on the ground with one arm outstretched as if he were reaching for something. For what, his mother couldn't say, because there was nothing close by to reach for. Perhaps, he was grasping for one last moment of life—a life ended all too soon.

Olive Dunford Drewes had begun her journey west more than a week before. She had read in the papers about the strike. She had wondered why her son had not written. She had hoped to step in and stop any trouble before things got out of hand.

She had arrived that very morning. But her visit was too late. It was too late to save lives, but not too late, she vowed, to make things better.

Olive took the journal from her son's cold hand. It was opened to a yellowed page. The page was torn. The date of the entry was August 21, 1853. Hattie's handwriting was rough. Olive read:

"Thomas and I have been traveling for some time now. I look forward to my new life with him in South Carolina. But I do miss the West! And how I miss brother Matthew, mother, and father. As we move on I see more and more of this country. It is a huge land. Open and wide and free. It is full of beginnings and endings. Full of life and death.

"One man comes in. He plants and builds a home. Then another comes along and builds nearby. Soon towns spring up where once there were tepees. Roads cover old wooded paths. Life is destroyed to make way for new life. Sometimes I get dizzy thinking about it all. Life here seems to move faster with every passing minute.

"But I will never forget that people make the land what it is. Their actions speak for them. I hope that they will always act for the right and for the good. Then, no matter what changes come, I know they will be changes for the better."

Olive closed Hattie's journal. Then she picked up Harry's journal from the rubble. She clutched both books close to her heart.

Olive stood and said a prayer, a prayer for Harry and for Hattie. Then she said a prayer for all the people who had died.

And finally she prayed for the living— for herself and for the workers—and for all those who would come after them.

"Changes for the better," she said aloud. "Yes. I promise you that, Harry Drewes. I promise you that."